AF316652

The Epistles

Waqar Faiz

Dedication

All praise is due to the One before all, the Lord of all, the Creator of All, the One who is beyond all conceptualization, then even beyond that, then even beyond that. It is to Him I dedicate this work, to all of His chosen servants, His friends, and those who follow their path.

Table Of Contents

Preface

What is my purpose? Why do I exist? These questions serve as guideposts for the human experience. Curiosity fuels the exploration and study of creation. However, as a person goes further into this journey of exploration, other questions arise. Why do we question existence and its purpose? Why do we seek more clarity in the face of these questions? This line of inquiry fuels a spiritual exploration. I have found many answers to these questions after walking the path, and I have elected to relay some of them in these words to you.

My friends, we tend to live cyclical lives, trying to understand everything at once only to be right back where we started. This work is a set of letters providing wisdom from my own experiences when confronted with truth and reality. As for you, my dear friends, take your time with these words. Examine these words deeply and give yourselves time to witness them at work in your life. You no doubt have your own questions about life and existence that you would like answered. Do not worry; you are not alone in your quest. I am here to tell you that it is all part of the path, and if you remain consistent in your search for the truth, you, too, will find answers.

Just as my guide enlightened me, I endeavor to relay some of the wisdom I have received to you. However, do not merely take in this wisdom with your eyes but imbue it within your heart and soul. Use these words as a source to embrace what wisdom you can glean. My friends, let us not waste our time on this earth. We can deny many things, but we cannot deny death and its inevitable approach. So, use your time wisely, and you will see how beautiful life can be when you understand yourself and your place in the universe.

Author's Bio

Waqar Faiz was born in the city of Lahore. His mother provided his early education, instilling in him a love of the Creator and a desire to reflect on His message. Later in life, Waqar Faiz spontaneously experienced a powerful spiritual state. Seeking to be closer to the Divine and His Messenger ﷺ, he would pray hundreds of prayers every day. Seeking guidance, he found a spiritual mentor in Sayyid Mahmud Ali Shah, who would pass away soon after.

At this point, Waqar Faiz began to receive spiritual instructions via dreams. After following the instructions given in the dreams, he would find the dreams to be true. He began to meet with different spiritual masters who would offer him spiritual knowledge and instruction. This was the start of a tremendous spiritual journey that continues to this day.

Through this connection, constant spiritual exercise, physical retreats into the wilderness, and unflinching service to humanity, Waqar Faiz honed and deepened his connection to the Divine. This connection became so deep that Waqar Faiz entered into a state of spirituality that allowed him to witness the secrets of the Divine Essence, leading to an intimate understanding of the wisdom behind Divine correspondence.

Waqar Faiz currently resides in Houston, Texas. He provides assistance and service to people all over the world and has taken on the mission of imparting these wisdoms to seekers. His guidance provides a means of connection not just to the realm of spirituality but also to the Creator Himself, enabling seekers to walk the spiritual path with serenity, humility, and submission.

Part One:

TRUTH

First Letter – News

News, stark and austere,
A deterrent tale did weave,
Hearts quiver in fear.

Humans have encountered extraordinary phenomena throughout history. These events are profound windows into the truth of the universe and a testament to our journey of discovery. These remarkable events hold undeniable truths, yet the spiritually deficient choose to ignore them.

Pride and stubbornness influence their refusal. Witnesses reject the extraordinary event and its truth. They attribute it to trickery to discredit the source and its purpose.

This rejection is not solely due to intellectual doubts. It is a reflection of their inclinations and motivations. Temporal pursuits drive them. They cling to their status quo and resist any challenge to their established misconceptions and ways of life. In doing so, they dismiss these signs as illusions and deception, only to stay complacent and avoid change.

In essence, they dismiss what is beyond logic and attribute it to deceit. This highlights the reality of human nature. People reject what contradicts their desires, even when faced with evidence. The spiritually enlightened will value the importance of humility, open-mindedness, and sincerity. They understand the harm of letting biases and attachments obstruct the ability to see the truth.

Second Letter – Skeptics

Skeptics, heed Our Decree,
Prior commands now forbid,
Self-wrong, not from Us.

People bring about their own discontent when they abandon their adopted principles. They are fully aware of their denial. Yet, they choose to be skeptical. They seek comfort in their skepticism despite once claiming to understand and accept reality. Their deliberate denial of truth results in significant consequences in the future.

The pursuit of temporary pleasures at the expense of perpetual gratification is a grave error. The spiritually deficient opt for temporary happiness over lasting contentment. In doing so, they effectively forfeit everlasting benefits. They exchange truth for the mundane. This choice reveals misplaced priorities and a lack of inspiration.

Their arrogance hinders them from turning back to their path. They have blunted their own senses, and they bar themselves from what is ultimately good. They possess the ability to comprehend but choose to remain ignorant of the outcomes of their choices.

The spiritually enlightened emphasize the need to stay committed to one's principles. They avoid the allure of the mundane, knowing that it risks true prosperity. They remain cognizant of the consequences of knowingly rejecting the truth. They will always display real dedication to principles of integrity.

Third Letter – They Cry

They cry out,
Reflect, will you not, they're urged,
Silent hearts remain.

Fairness is evident in life and death with respect to a person's assigned tasks. In this world, justice is upheld by not burdening anyone beyond their capacity. Each person has tasks assigned to them well within their capabilities, ensuring an equitable approach.

Accountability for actions is paramount. Every action, regardless of its magnitude, remains in the record of the universe. People cannot avoid the truth. Every part of a person's life is documented, reflecting their choices and intentions.

Justice dictates that individuals receive compensation or consequences based on their efforts. It will recognize those who acted with integrity. Those who defied will face repercussions. The spiritually enlightened share a commitment to justice. They work to ensure fairness prevails for all.

Fourth Letter – Intoxicants

Intoxicants, games,
Vice and value entwined,
Excess, wisdom guides.

The spiritually enlightened avoid certain acts for their own benefit. People often question why certain things are taboo and seek understanding. There is always wisdom behind avoiding prohibited acts. Initially, such things may have been allowed to some extent. However, when their misuse began to harm society, such acts could no longer hold any place in it.

These acts may seem attractive, but only outwardly. They may offer short-term benefits but cause significant long-term harm. They have detrimental effects on both individuals and society. The spiritually enlightened direct their thoughts toward long-term consequences. They value the long term over immediate gratification when making decisions. They strive to reflect moral integrity. They work to abstain from actions that cause harm or are immoral.

The spiritually enlightened never shy away from charity. Furthermore, they advise others to give from their surplus to help those in need. They foster values of generosity and compassion while ensuring individuals maintain their well-being.

Fifth Letter – Scripture's People

Scripture's people, heed,
Truth in doctrine, declare,
Real Oneness, revere.

Spiritual openings relate to the concept of unity. Every opening will illuminate its different levels. Those who witness these openings focus on the truth and avoid falsehoods.

Their method is to avoid extreme practice. They adopt moderation and sincerity. They adhere to principles of truthfulness in devotion and actions.

The essence of a spiritual opening is reliance on the spiritually enlightened. They have an important role and a profound connection to the truth. Having witnessed true unity, they work to uphold it by negating all aspects of multiplicity or partnership in true oneness. Their adherence to oneness reflects the high caliber of their nature and relationship to the ultimate reality.

The spiritually enlightened will affirm and reaffirm unity. They emphasize the uniqueness and incomparability of this truth. They negate any associate, emphasizing the oneness of the ultimate reality and its importance.

Sixth Letter – People of Lore

People of old Lore,
Truth and falsehood intertwined,
Why hide what is true?

The spiritually enlightened encourage people from different backgrounds to find common ground. They should seek to understand the truth. Sincere communication prompts reflection and dialogue. It emphasizes honesty and clarity in principles and actions.

It is important to acknowledge truth and avoid falsehood. One who does this will acquire the integrity needed in important matters. Furthermore, they will encourage honesty and sincerity in intentions and actions.

The spiritually deficient conceal the truth. They do so due to personal biases, vested interests, or ignorance. The spiritually enlightened emphasize openness and transparency, even if it challenges current ideas.

In addition, the spiritually enlightened invite others of diverse backgrounds to take part in constructive dialogue and mutual understanding.

This fosters respect, tolerance, and cooperation among different communities. It promotes greater harmony and peaceful coexistence.

Dialogue must always be tempered with truth and clarity. People must be honest and seek truth earnestly. They should also engage politely with others, no matter their background. These principles promote a dedication to the truth that extends to all communities.

Seventh Letter – Dominion

*Dominion rules
those who tread the path alone,
and those who stray, lost.*

A cornerstone of the spiritual path is the principle of responsibility and accountability in personal matters. It stresses that individuals alone are responsible for their understanding, actions, and outcomes. It emphasizes that people have authority only over themselves. It highlights the importance of personal accountability for one's intentions and actions. The path also stresses personal freedom and independence. It does so in both principle and practice. It shows that each person is accountable for the direction they choose to take. Those who walk the path do not force their views or choices on others.

The path also advocates universal fairness. Each person has an individual responsibility, even if everyone believes or acts differently. The spiritually enlightened prompt us to consider the importance of being genuine and diligent in our own matters. They encourage people to think about their beliefs and actions. They impart the awareness that each person alone must face the outcomes of their decisions. They motivate people to pursue virtue and truth in their spiritual efforts.

Eighth Letter – Livestock

Livestock, varied roles,
Transport, clothing, sustenance,
Value nature's gifts

The spiritually enlightened embody spiritual discipline through conscientious dietary choices. Proper food consumption instills humility and mindfulness in daily life. The wisdoms that guide dietary discipline include hygienic considerations. The wise will make choices that are of physical and spiritual benefit. The spiritually enlightened follow these guidelines in their roles as stewards of the natural world. They treat other living creatures with compassion and use the Earth's resources carefully. The guidelines for food consumption have many spiritual and physical advantages. They also uphold the sanctity of creation and foster unity in the community. These dietary principles are key to living a peaceful, harmonious life. They bring one into conformity with natural law. Following these guidelines brings awareness of the magnitude of nature. Its system is best suited to us in that it dwarfs all alternatives. The spiritually enlightened adhere to the natural order within the universe. They are intimately aware that nature serves humanity's needs. Thus, they strive to use nature's resources wisely.

Ninth Letter – Schemes

Schemes come to naught then,
No aid shall their efforts find,
Judgment stands alone.

The spiritually deficient become objects of retribution. They must face the consequences of arrogance and haughtiness. Eventually, they are overtaken by their past misdeeds. Their pleas for help fall on deaf ears. Accountability is inevitable. Those who reject truth cannot escape the consequences of their actions.

Arrogance and heedlessness are spiritual diseases whose main symptom is the opposition to guidance. Efforts to oppose guidance are utterly pointless, and the consequences are ultimately unavoidable. The spiritually diseased try to find refuge from their impending doom. They plead and appeal, but they find themselves helpless and abandoned. They face the full force of justice.

True power is the triumph of truth over falsehood. This victory is the principle that will prevail. Judgment in this matter is swift and just. The spiritually enlightened remind us of the importance of humility, obedience, and faithfulness in the face of fate. The spiritually deficient reflect the dire results of defiance and rebellion against reality.

Tenth Letter – Power

Power commands winds,
Clouds stir over barren land,
Life springs from the dust.

The spiritually enlightened respect the delicate balance of nature. They reflect on the signs of true power in the universe. A simple yet powerful example of this is how nature sends down water from the sky, filling valleys and allowing vegetation to come to life. This process is vital for life on Earth. Water is essential for all plants, and plants support ecosystems and provide sustenance for other living creatures. Wisdom is also often represented as water, giving way to spiritual life.

The spiritually enlightened remind us of the role of water in the cycle of life. They highlight its power to revive barren land and bring forth vegetation. This takes place in our lives daily, yet we often overlook how miraculous this is. The natural world shows us instances of the dead coming back to life. Through this imagery, the spiritually enlightened invite us to reflect on the power and wisdom in the universe. The universe comprises the natural world's intricate workings with precision and purpose.

Furthermore, the spiritually enlightened share their awareness of the power that is evident in sustaining and renewing the Earth. They showcase the mercy and generosity by which this world is sustained. They themselves reflect and encourage contemplation on the signs of true existence and strength in nature. They enjoy the beauty and harmony of creation. Through this simple example of water, they convey the countless wisdoms that flow from it.

Eleventh Letter – Love Wealth

Love wealth so immense,
Greed's hunger knows no limit,
Empty hearts still ache.

The spiritually deficient have abandoned certain principles. The spiritually enlightened caution us that those who abandon their principles will fall prey to the outcomes of their actions. They remind us that people will directly experience the repercussions of their past. Thus, they encourage accountability and justice. People are responsible for their choices and actions. The spiritually enlightened remind us that one cannot escape the consequences of their behavior and stress the need for ethical conduct and responsibility in life.

Twelfth Letter – Indulging

Indulging with those,
In shared moments, we revel,
Memories remain.

The spiritually enlightened are called to convey a message to others, leaving those people to decide whether to accept or reject it. Pure souls remind us of the freedom of choice individuals have in matters of life. Everyone receives guidance, but each person must decide whether to accept or reject it. The spiritually enlightened underscore the importance of individual autonomy and responsibility in all matters.

Thirteenth Letter – In Sleep's Embrace

In sleep's embrace, signs,
Day and night, bounty pursued,
For those who heed, signs.

The spiritually enlightened remind us of two important facets of human life: sleep and the effort to secure sustenance. They view sleep as a natural rhythm that suggests a guiding force. This force guides the alternating states of wakefulness and rest. They also acknowledge the human drive to procure sustenance. They view this drive, in turn, as evidence of a generous provision in existence.

Moreover, they see these experiences as indicators for those who are observant and thoughtful of a deeper spiritual truth. By looking at sleep patterns and the search for sustenance, individuals may see signs of a higher power. They may perceive its presence and qualities. This is why the spiritually enlightened remind us of the importance of reflection and awareness. In doing so, we may see signs of the existence and kindness of that higher power in the world.

Fourteenth Letter – Obey

Obey the decree,
Messenger's guidance embraced,
Mercy shall follow.

The spiritually enlightened stress the need to follow spiritual teachings and guidance. They stress that such obedience and respect are vital for spiritual growth and receiving mercy. By following their teachings and emulating a guide who embodies them, individuals can unearth the most beautiful intentions. This, in turn, makes them receptive to infinite compassion.

They also inform us that obedience goes beyond mere compliance. They show a path to seeking mercy and its source. They highlight the close link between obedience and kindness and show that those who obey are more attuned to the favor and compassion they receive.

In essence, the enlightened prompt seekers to focus on adhering to guidance. They should do so as a means to attain special mercy and finally achieve spiritual fulfillment.

Fifteenth Letter – Mercy

Mercy from beyond,
The Hearer, Knower of all,
Infinite grace, yours.

The spiritually enlightened practice patience in the face of criticism and adversity. In every state, they praise and give gratitude to a higher power. This is especially so during various times of the day and night. Admitting the greatness of a higher power and giving thanks often gives rise to profound satisfaction. It can also lead to contentment in life. The enlightened stress the importance of resilience, spiritual reflection, and gratitude. They help in navigating life's challenges and finding inner peace and fulfillment.

Sixteenth Letter – Inspired

Inspired by Soul,
Guiding lights walk among us,
Seek wisdom to know.

Pure souls reflect a consistent historical trend of communication from higher realms. They inform that the Divine Entity, the higher power of the cosmos and beyond, sent human emissaries to convey guidance. They were human beings who walked among us. However, they received revelations and conveyed them to their communities.

The spiritually enlightened remind us to reflect and use simple logic in daily matters. They remind us of the harm suffered by past societies that rejected their advice. They prompt people to think about the results of their actions. They also hold space for others to think about the messages conveyed by these people.

The enlightened also inform of the reality of honor for those who prioritize guidance. They remind us that those who uphold these principles will find ultimate fulfillment.

Seventeenth Letter – At The Fork

At the fork they stood,
Their fish forgotten, it slipped,
Into the river.

Two travelers arrive at a junction between two bodies of water. They continue on their path. However, they unintentionally leave behind the fish they had brought for their meal. Surprisingly, the fish comes to life and finds its way back into the water. It slips away without notice.

The forgotten fish's tale illustrates the emanation of deep wisdom and guidance. This wisdom even surpasses what humans can understand. It sets the stage for a seeker's encounter with their guide. During it, the traveler gains insights into patience and wisdom and learns the deep mysteries of providence.

The spiritually enlightened prompt contemplation about the unforeseen ways that deep wisdom shows itself in our lives. They remind us of the importance of staying open to guidance and knowledge. They serve as guides to go beyond what we immediately understand.

Eighteenth Letter – Gradually Near

Gradually near,
Returning to the great source,
Fading from our sight.

The spiritually enlightened offer insight into the gradual revelation of guidance. In response to those who question its pace, they relay that truth unfolds at its own pace. This process strengthens and transforms people over time. It fosters spiritual growth and understanding. In a broader context, it shows the purposeful nature of guidance. The goal is to nurture humanity's spiritual journey and prompt reflection. There is deep wisdom in slowly revealing true knowledge that shapes humanity's path to enlightenment.

Nineteenth Letter – Do We Not Recall?

Do we not recall?
Before existence, we came,
From void to being.

The divinely inspired ones encourage deep consideration of the profound origins of human existence. They prompt us to ponder whether we know our humble beginnings. We often lose sight of this reality despite it.

In a broader sense, they invite reflection on the amazing journey of human development. This journey goes from a single cell to a complex entity. They remind us of the inherent wisdom and power in the creation of each individual.

The enlightened remind us to acknowledge and value the origin and purpose of human life. This will inspire humility and gratitude as we

contemplate the miraculous journey of existence.

Twentieth Letter – From Skies

From skies, water falls,
Rivers flow within their bounds,
Truth in froth's display.

The spiritually enlightened employ the imagery of falling rain and flowing rivers to convey a spiritual message. They describe how rainfall fills valleys to their capacity, and a froth forms as the water flows. Similarly, when metals melt in fire to make ornaments or utensils, a similar froth appears on the surface. The froth is merely temporary, while that which lies beneath it gives true benefit.

They draw a parallel between these natural events and truth and falsehood. They stress the brief nature of deceit, like the fleeting foam. In contrast, truth endures and gives lasting benefits, just as what remains after the froth dissipates.

In essence, this natural phenomenon serves as a reminder of the enduring nature of truth and the impermanence of falsehood. It prompts reflection about the results of your actions and choices. It shows the importance of aligning with truth, which brings lasting benefit to yourself and others.

Twenty-First Letter – Bounty Spreads

Bounty spreads, unfurls,
Yet most remain unaware,
Lord's will, vast and veiled.

The spiritually enlightened remind us that the Divine Entity alone has authority over the sustenance and support of people. The Divine distributes the provision as He sees fit. The Divine also ensures that any resources spent in His service will be repaid. This reaffirms the kindness and care of the Divine Entity toward creation.

The enlightened promote confidence in the wisdom and care of the Divine. They remind us that this Entity is the true source of sustenance and support. The Divine Entity meets people's needs and honors their efforts. The spiritually enlightened remind us to foster an appreciation for and reliance on the kindness and abundance of the Divine.

Twenty-Second Letter – Accept

Accept, then reject,
Deeper into darkness plunged,
Lost, repentance fades.

The spiritually enlightened caution against the serious consequences faced by those who once subscribed to a set of principles. They renounced those principles and deepened their unbelief. After passing from this existence, their attempts at reconciliation will not be acknowledged. The severity of their actions and the extent of their deviation serve as a barrier between them and the Divine.

This shows the importance of adhering to one's beliefs and the serious results of betrayal. It also stresses maintaining a sincere commitment to one's principles. It shows the dangers of departing from them.

Twenty-Third Letter – In Prayer

In prayer, they bow,
Heart's whispers to the Divine,
Seeking grace and peace.

The spiritually enlightened remind us of the commencement of divine revelation and the profound impact of divine guidance on humanity. They emphasize the Creator's identity as the ultimate source of knowledge. The Creator imparts wisdom that was previously unknown to humanity.

The enlightened highlight the importance of divine revelation. It is a means of enlightenment and guidance for humanity. It shows the power of knowledge and stresses the need to seek understanding throughout life.

The enlightened remind us of the Divine's key role in educating and enlightening humanity. They encourage people to seek further wisdom and guidance from the Divine.

Twenty-Fourth Letter –
Believers

Believers, make space,
Mercy's hold widens for you,
Disperse, rise in faith.

The spiritually enlightened guide people on how to behave at gatherings and meetings in their community. They show the importance of cooperation and compliance and urge seekers to accommodate others when asked and to leave when necessary.

Furthermore, they remind us that the Divine will honor believers who follow these guidelines. This is especially true for those who are entrenched in faith and knowledge. This honor depicts an advancement in status, sometimes reflected by one's position within the community.

The enlightened stress cooperation, obedience, and modesty within the community. They also highlight the importance of honoring good etiquette. They promise divine recognition for those who do so, especially for the paragons of faith and knowledge.

Twenty-Fifth Letter – The Living

The Living, alone,
Pray, devotion pure, for One
Praise the Source of All.

The spiritually enlightened present that the core belief of the path is in the existence of a singular, living Creator. They encourage people to offer their prayers only to the One Creator with utmost sincerity and commitment. They constantly and consistently offer praise and thanks to the Source, recognizing His sovereignty over all existence.

They reinforce the key concept of monotheism and stress the value of earnest devotion to the Divine Entity alone. They remind people to keep this belief of Oneness in their worship and to show gratitude for all blessings to that ultimate sustainer of all existence.

Twenty-Sixth Letter – Peace

Peace upon their birth,
And upon their final day,
And when they're revived.

The spiritually enlightened constantly extend wishes of peace to the chosen servants of the Divine. They speak of their birth, their passing, and their resurrection.

The mention of peace at their birth signifies the tranquility and blessings of their arrival. Similarly, peace when they pass on denotes a calm departure from earthly life. Peace when they rise shows the mercy and favor given to them in all phases of their existence.

The enlightened speak of the extraordinary life, passing, and resurrection of these beautiful individuals. They remind us of the unique divine attention and status given to these chosen servants of the Divine.

Twenty-Seventh Letter – Spouses

Spouses and children,
Grant us joy, be our model,
For virtue, we pray.

Pure souls offer prayers for blessings within their familial relationships. They seek companions and children who bring them joy and fulfillment. This is symbolized as "the coolness of our eyes." Additionally, they eagerly seek to manifest virtuous behavior for the benefit of believers. They express their desire to serve as moral guides.

Humanity occupies itself with many concerns. These include personal happiness within their lives and families. However, the pure-hearted are also concerned with their broader societal duty as moral exemplars. Harmonious families are important in this dynamic as well. The pure-hearted and their intimate companions desire to set good examples through values like empathy, integrity, and leadership.

Twenty-Eighth Letter – Blessed

Blessed, he withdraws,
In hardship, despair takes hold,
Humanity's plight.

It is typical human behavior that when people receive blessings or prosperity, they often become indifferent. They distance themselves from the origin of their blessings and focus on themselves. However, in hard times, they become desperate. In such moments, they seek solace through prayer.

This offers insight into human habits. Those engulfed in unawareness will switch between indifference and desperation. Their attitude changes with the situation. The spiritually enlightened stress the importance of gratitude alongside resilience in both favorable and challenging situations. They encourage individuals to embrace humility and acknowledge their innate dependence upon the Divine. They remind us to hold fast to this truth regardless of circumstances.

Twenty-Ninth Letter – Love

Love for fleeting life,
Leaves weighty Day in its wake,
Choices carve their path.

The spiritually enlightened remind us that the majority of future outcomes depend on people's actions and efforts in this life. Divine justice is the crux of this truth. People will receive honor or debasement based on their actions.

They stress the significance of human responsibility and accountability. They remind people that their choices and efforts in life shape their fate long after this life ends. So, they encourage people to manifest virtuous behavior, thereby drawing ever closer to the Divine. Thus, the Divine recognizes and honors their efforts.

Thirtieth Letter – Mountains

Mountains like wool tufts,
Earth's grandeur humbled to naught,
Time's vast sweep revealed.

The arrival of the Day of Judgement is heralded by a significant transformation in the Heavens. It is described as the sky taking on the appearance of murky oil, suggesting a profound alteration in its nature as well as its function.

This arrival signifies the unfathomable power of the Divine Entity. This power manifests throughout all the awe-inspiring events that will transpire on this day. The spiritually enlightened remind us that the material world is impermanent and that the Divine has absolute sovereignty over all existence.

Thirty-First Letter – Signs

Signs recited, pride,
Deafness veils the truth's clear call,
Painful warning sounds.

The spiritually deficient are examples of negative reactions to guidance. They display haughty disregard for the message and its bearer. They embody deafness in both sound and heart by choosing to ignore and reject the truth.

Their example serves as a cautionary tale. It illustrates the results of obstinately rejecting guidance from the Divine. It exhibits the results of arrogance and disbelief. The spiritually enlightened emphasize the importance of humility and receptiveness to the Divine message, for its disregard could very well lead to severe consequences in the future.

Thirty-Second Letter – Believers Mindful

Believers mindful,
Guided by faith, wisdom's light,
Their path unfolds clear.

The spiritually enlightened clearly depict the traits of believers. They have unwavering conviction in the Divine Entity. They carefully consider their behavior and strive to uphold moral integrity and virtue.

Their appraisal of these traits is an expression of the core tenets of faith and moral uprightness. They highlight the importance of believing in the Divine and of being mindful of one's actions. The enlightened encourage people to live in devotion to truth and reality. They guide others to a path of spiritual growth and a deeper connection to the Divine.

Thirty-Third Letter – Magicians

Magicians bow low,
Recognizing truth's decree,
Humbled by its glow.

A messenger arrives with divine correspondence. A group initially in denial of his authority witness an astonishing display of divine power. They acknowledge the truth when faced with clear evidence and bow in reverence, affirming their faith in the Divine.

This tale shows the power of faith and the deep impact of witnessing a miraculous event. It shows how encountering extraordinary signs of the Divine can prompt profound transformation. In this way, even enemies can forsake negative allegiances and embrace belief in the Divine Entity alone.

Thirty-Fourth Letter – Death's Decree

Death's decree proclaimed,
Immutable fate ordained,
None can elude it.

Humanity has an intimate link with the Divine. This relationship exists whether or not we are aware of it. The Divine Entity has a presence that reaches far beyond human awareness.

The enlightened emphasize the certainty of death and its inevitable encounter. They encourage others to reflect on the fleeting nature of life and the importance of preparing for the afterlife. They urge people to acknowledge the nearness of the Creator and lead their lives with an ever-growing awareness of His presence. Souls purified in this manner constantly seek His guidance and compassion.

Thirty-Fifth Letter – Time's Sudden Approach

Time's sudden approach,
Tokens foretold, yet ignored,
Message unheeded.

The Divine has kept a time in which all shall end and return to life. The resurrected will be gathered to review the sum total of their deeds. They will face a final determination on the life that they lived. The spiritually enlightened prompt us to reflect on the signs of this impending significant event. These signs are present in the natural world, like the intricate design and beauty of the Heavens. They are a clear indication for those who take notice. They remind us of the inevitable arrival of this important moment.

They sincerely advise people to reflect on the message of that Day's arrival. Pure souls accept the reality of the coming event before its abrupt occurrence. The enlightened stress the need to remain vigilant and prepared for the hereafter rather than postponing recognition until it is too late.

Thirty-Sixth Letter – Master

Master of all realms,
Heaven, earth, and what lies 'tween,
Lord of many Easts.

The spiritually enlightened highlight the supremacy and transcendence of the Divine. They declare that the Divine is the Creator and Caretaker of the Heavens, the Earth, and everything in between. The Divine has total control over all existence. His rule transcends all directions. His authority extends to every region and domain, known and unknown, perceived and imperceptible.

This portrayal presents the Creator as the highest authority and that His control extends over every particle of creation. This includes the vast celestial realms and the smallest details of earthly life. It evokes awe and reverence for this power. Pure souls are transformed in their acknowledgment of the Creator's absolute omnipotence.

Thirty-Seventh Letter – Leave Me

Leave Me with the one
Its affair, its Judgment, Mine
I created Alone.

The spiritually enlightened advise believers to have patience and trust in the Divine. This is necessary, especially when faced with rejection. Denial typically comes from those who enjoy worldly blessings but deny them to others and reject divine correspondence. The enlightened advise leaving the matter to the Divine, who allows deniers time before facing repercussions.

They remind believers to persevere in spreading their message, even in the face of rejection and opposition. They promote reliance on divine providence. The Divine has promised His judgment to all, especially persistent deniers, despite their worldly comfort.

Thirty-Eighth Letter – He Said

He said, "Thus decrees
Your Lord: 'It's easy for Me,
A mercy, a sign.'"

An angel conveys the Divine decree of a miraculous birth of a child to a chosen servant. This narrative underscores the ease with which the Creator executes plans and the special significance of the child's birth as a sign of mercy from the Divine to humanity.

It highlights the reassurance of the Divine's close supervision of human affairs, symbolized by the miraculous birth of the child. It signifies the Divine power to manifest signs and extend mercy to humanity, all according to the Divine decree.

Thirty-Ninth Letter – Good News

Good news in this life,
And in the hereafter, too.
the Divine's words true.

The spiritually enlightened address the importance of conveying the Divine message to people. This message conveys truth and reality, bringing people good news for both their worldly lives and the hereafter. The enlightened emphasize divine wisdom's eternal truth and reliability, holding that it remains unchanged. They stress the ultimate success of following divine guidance by assuring believers of blessings in this life and the hereafter. This reinforces the concept of ultimate reality, the immutability of divine decree, and the unassailable nature of divine wisdom.

Fortieth Letter – Craft Armor

Craft armor with care,
Measure each link with virtue.
the Divine observes.

The enlightened embody a balanced approach to life. Armor is a reference to physical and spiritual preparation for the struggles one may face on the path. They follow the path of ethical conduct coupled with thoughtful planning and scrupulousness. When this method is followed, the soul undergoes purification. A person becomes aware of the Creator's authority and knowledge. Eventually, they perceive His awareness over every action.

Those purified in this manner realize that associating partners with the Divine is futile. They arrive at the conclusion that there is no power or strength except with the Creator. They fully embrace the reality of monotheism and acknowledge the Divine's sole authority over all creation. The enlightened guide ultimately to the exclusive sovereignty and uniqueness of the Divine Entity, without any partners or rivals.

Forty-First Letter – Justice

On Day of Justice,
They'll enter the realm prepared.
Awaiting their fate.

The differences between people based on their beliefs and actions will be very apparent on the Day of Judgment. People who uphold what is right and embrace the truth will enter into perpetual grace and honor. Those who did wrong and denied the truth will face debasement and loss of dignity.

Servants of the Divine have always underscored the idea of human accountability. They have instilled in others the Divine principle of justice. According to this principle, people are repaid for their deeds and beliefs. In terms of accountability, there is no greater significance than the Day of Judgment.

As such, the Divine has proclaimed the destiny of the pure and enlightened. He affirms that they will attain everlasting bliss and joy in the afterlife. This is the result of their virtuous conduct and unwavering conviction.

Forty-Second Letter – Blessed Book

Blessed Book descends,
For pondering its message,
Wisdom for the wise.

The highest form of Divine Correspondence is revealed scripture. The Divine has gifted it to aid in deep thought and self-reflection. Divine Speech adjures people to ponder deeply. It offers guidance and profound wisdom for those with intellect at every level.

The enlightened emphasize the importance of engaging with the Creator's commands. Those seeking enlightenment realize that revealed scripture is more than just recitation or memorization. It is a fountainhead of deep knowledge and insight. Those seeking purity and enlightenment must use their minds and hearts to grasp the truths hidden in its messages.

Moreover, the wise will strictly adhere to the teachings of revealed scripture as they have realized the value of its lessons. Revealed scripture offers guidance in its every letter, but only those who are open to its message can fully take it.

Forty-Third Letter – No Sustenance

No sustenance sought,
Nor reliance on their care,
Independent, free.

The enlightened introduce the Divine Entity as absolutely One and completely Self-Sufficient. The Divine is the Creator and Sustainer of all existence. He does not need sustenance or provision. He is sovereign and independent. He is free from all outside sources for existence.

The enlightened remind humanity of their inescapable reliance on the Creator for all their needs and sustenance. They instill in others the acknowledgment of the Divine's self-sufficiency and providence. This acknowledgment unlocks the station of humility. It bolsters trust in the Divine in every aspect of life.

Ultimately, those seeking purity and enlightenment illuminate their hearts with the belief in the Creator's transcendence and self-sufficiency. They build their trust in divine providence and submit to the Creator's will.

Forty-Fourth Letter – One

One reigns over all,
Guardians watch us till death,
Angels claim the soul.

Spiritual deficiency arises from the denial of truth despite seeing miraculous signs and clear evidence. Its major symptom is the stubbornness of those who persist in disbelief. They do so even when undeniable proof of the Divine's existence and message is shown. The spiritually deficient come face to face with disaster due to their rejection of divine guidance.

Spiritual enlightenment arises from the fundamental principles of divine guidance and human accountability. It finds its source in the existence of the Creator. The Creator guides whom He wills and allows others to stray. The signs of His guidance can be found based in part on people's response to His message. This message is a reminder to the human soul of the importance of belief in the Divine and obeying His commands. It also informs of the results of ignoring guidance.

Moreover, it offers insights into the mercy and justice of the Divine. The Divine provides guidance to humanity but allows them the freedom to choose their own paths. Those who opt to reject guidance do so at their own peril. They face the consequences of their decisions both here and after this life ends.

Forty-Fifth Letter – Past Tales

Past tales are unveiled,
Unknown to you and your kin,
Pious are patient.

The Divine's chosen servants work diligently to convey the message of the Creator. They bring people to the path of turning back to the Creator and elevating their behavior. They teach the reality of the Creator's Oneness and unveil secrets of enlightenment. However, the communities of these servants from previous times often persisted in stubborn disbelief, dismissing both messenger and message.

Their stories serve as moral lessons that underscore the harm of spurning divine guidance and persisting in harmful behavior. Their example highlights the importance of heeding the advice of the chosen servants of the Divine. The messengers teach us to recognize signs of the Divine. They show us how to realize our connection with Him before this life draws to a close. The examples of previous civilizations who denied the message are a timeless reminder of the outcomes of arrogance, disobedience, and the rejection of truth.

Forty-Sixth Letter – As Daylight Fades

As the daylight fades,
Pray until night's deep embrace,
At dawn, Divine's grace.

When the Divine's chosen servants convey His message, they place great importance on critical thinking. The ability to think for oneself is key in matters of belief. Moreover, the Divine's chosen messengers appeal to rational thought to demonstrate the absurdity of idol worship. Finally, they bring people to enlightenment through sincere devotion to the Divine Entity alone.

These messengers faced resistance and challenges when conveying the Divine's message to their societies. However, they were resolute in their mission of calling people to worship the one true Creator.

Those seeking purity and enlightenment emulate the Divine's chosen servants. They uphold monotheism, using reason to identify truth. The enlightened do not abandon critical thinking and firm belief in difficult times.

Forty-Seventh Letter – Amidst

Amidst the turmoil,
No solace found in friendship,
Each to face alone.

The Day of Judgement exhibits human behavior in challenging circumstances. Individuals on the Day of Judgment will feel fear and anxiety in their hearts as they witness its events. On that day, each person will be concerned with himself, and no bonds of family or friendship will be of any significance. As such, people will experience intense emotions while reviewing their own deeds amidst the cosmic turmoil on the Day of Resurrection.

This Day of Judgment is inevitable. Its deep impact on humanity is an inescapable truth. Its reality is that all will be held accountable for their actions. Pure souls strive to lead an ethical life to prepare for the hereafter. The enlightened are aware of how fleeting worldly concerns are. These concerns are but a drop in the ocean compared to the eternal results awaiting humanity.

Those seeking purity reflect on the shortness of worldly pleasures and the everlasting nature of the hereafter. Those seeking enlightenment will prioritize their spiritual development. Such people prepare for the Day of Judgment by fostering firm belief, elevated behavior, and devotion to the Divine.

Forty-Eighth Letter – In The Quiet

In the quiet night,
They bow in deep reverence,
Seeking their Lord's grace.

Those seeking to complete their purity spend their nights in prayer, seeking deep spiritual connection to the Divine. Their commitment to this nightly worship is a symbol of humility and dedication to a higher purpose. This practice invites introspection, contemplation during quiet moments, and removing oneself from distractions.

Prayer and prostration at night symbolize respect for life's mysteries. They reflect a desire to grow and understand. These practices are a matrix for personal growth. They call on people to prioritize moments of reflection and self-improvement.

In essence, night worship encourages people to devote time to spiritual maturity. The Divine has gifted these practices to us as sources of well-being for all people.

Forty-Ninth Letter – Revelations

Revelations snubbed,
Divine warnings cast aside,
Justice will be served.

Disregarding divine guidance is the greatest injustice against the soul. The spiritually enlightened warn of the spiritual consequences of ignoring the Creator's reminders and revelations. The unenlightened are those who have not been exposed to such reminders. The spiritually deficient are those who neglect Divine guidance after becoming aware of it. This crime they commit against themselves is worse than any misdeed the unenlightened may commit.

The spiritually enlightened showcase the beauty and importance of heeding divine guidance. They steadfastly adhere to the Creator's revelations. They advise others to heed the repercussions of dismissing these reminders. The Divine Himself has stated that those who obstinately persist in such disregard will face consequences.

The enlightened prompt reflection on the principles of accountability and justice inherent in the Divine plan. Greater awareness of the Divine unlocks greater awareness of one's personal responsibility. Therefore, those seeking enlightenment will encounter greater responsibility with each advancing stage of their journey. Turning away from one's responsibility inflicts damage to the soul. Therefore, those who deliberately choose to turn away from the Divine's reminders will encounter increasing spiritual hardship.

We must answer for the harm we inflicted, not only on each other but on ourselves as well. Divine justice is guaranteed for every human soul. Those who harm themselves will face the results of that justice.

Fiftieth Letter – Wise

It is wise for them
Not to all march out all at once.
Let some stay behind,

Learn their faith deeply,
then share it then they return,
Spreading the pure light.

Those seeking to complete their purity approach all of their duties and responsibilities with a sense of balance. The enlightened advise such people to dedicate resources to ensure there are those in their communities who dedicate their time to deeply understanding divinely revealed principles. These individuals must deepen their understanding to enhance their knowledge and spiritual growth.

The enlightened encourage individual learning and reflection. However, they also stress the need for collective action and solidarity. Communities should always ensure that there are people who dedicate their time in this manner. These individuals have a role as educators and guides in their community. They help spread knowledge and, in turn, deepen their fellow community members' own understanding of divinely revealed principles.

There is practical wisdom behind this approach. By having a portion of dedicated people study these principles deeply, the community maintains continuity and stability. They can also warn and protect the community through their knowledge and guidance.

Fifty-First Letter – Assembly

Assembly of all,
Messengers warned, yet they strayed,
Worldly allure swayed.

The Divine has never left a single soul bereft of guidance. He has sent messengers to convey His revelations and to show a path that leads to His Essence. These messengers also warned their people of spiritually harmful behavior. This has all been conveyed as a clear and complete message. As such, the Divine will take people into account in the hereafter for the decisions they made in light of the guidance they received.

The act of sending these reputable souls as guides is an undeniable mercy from the Divine. He sent these chosen few to awaken people to their obligations, to warn them about the coming Day of Judgment, and to exemplify a moral life. Despite these warnings and reminders, some clung stubbornly to the attractions of worldly life and only deepened their disbelief and disobedience.

The spiritually enlightened reflect on divine communication with humanity. Guides imparted this knowledge across epochs, following these teachings and stressing the harm of neglecting them. Furthermore, the enlightened stress self-accountability. People will admit their own failings and disbelief on the Day of Judgment. They will serve as witnesses against themselves.

Fifty-Second Letter – Twisting

Twisting tongues deceive,
Scripture veiled in falsehood's guise,
Lies cloaked as divine.

The Divine has sent correspondence to creation in the form of revealed scripture. Those who adhered to the teachings of these scriptures in their original forms attained purity and enlightenment. However, the spiritually deficient sought to sully these scriptures with their own words. These are the worst of people. Their ego-driven manipulation leads to confusion and misunderstanding among those seeking to follow guidance. They alter the written form of these scriptures and portray their own interpretations as indisputable. This deceitful tactic leads others to accept their fabrications as genuine truths. The spiritually enlightened caution against people who manipulate teachings to suit their own interests. These corrupt individuals mislead others and sow discord within the group or community. The enlightened stress the need for careful analysis, critical thought, and most importantly, the guidance of enlightened souls when seeking to understand these teachings. They encourage those seeking guidance to stay vigilant against manipulation and falsehood.

Moreover, they emphasize the severity of falsely attributing statements to the Divine Entity. They highlight the ethical and moral duties tied to the teachings and rebuke those who knowingly deceive. They warn of the repercussions of this deception in this life and the next.

Fifty-Third Letter – Chains

Chains shattered, freedom,
From bondage to liberty,
Soul's liberation.

The spiritually enlightened guide to a path of striving toward integrity and spiritual growth. They remind us that a key principle of this path lies in the commitment to submission and moral excellence. Our souls are captives of our bodies, only to be set free when we break from the constraints of worldly attachments. The soul is always seeking true prosperity, which comes from the pursuit of truth and reality.

Those who neglect their spiritual growth and fail to follow divine guidance may become spiritually deprived and impoverished. Thus, the enlightened remind us of the value of ethical conduct and good character. It becomes clear that the ultimate outcome of good deeds is rooted in belief in the Divine Entity. A good deed lacking this belief is ultimately incomplete. There is no promise of any everlasting honor for such acts.

However, mere belief is not enough for purity and enlightenment. Those who have submitted to truth and reality must join with others who have also submitted, just as multiple streams flow into one large river. They should collectively strive to instill virtues in one another and remove vices as their path requires. Both the pure and enlightened prioritize their spiritual well-being and recognize the power of submission to the Divine to transform both individuals and society.

Fifty-Fourth Letter – Hypocrites

Hypocrites whisper,
Hearts diseased with dark deceit,
Rumors breed discord.

Among the spiritually deficient are those who spread rumors and discord to harm society's unity and stability. These are the people who portray themselves publicly as loyal but secretly are against truth and guidance.

Any community can face challenges from deceitful individuals. For example, in a workplace, some employees may say they support the organization's goals. However, they secretly act against the organization. They may spread rumors, manipulate situations, or incite conflicts to advance personal agendas. This disrupts workplace harmony and morale.

Similarly, in society, certain groups or people may exploit social media or other platforms. They use them to spread lies, stoke hatred, or promote divisive tales. Such activities can lead to polarization, erosion of trust, and even violence within communities.

In response, leaders may need to address the root causes of this discord. They may also need to confront those who spread lies or rumors. This may involve promoting transparency, enabling open dialogue, and fighting misinformation. It also involves fostering unity. However, no permanent resolution is possible without adhering to the principles of Divine guidance and reliance upon the Divine Entity.

In these situations, those who seek purity will be mindful of the importance of integrity, honesty, and solidarity. They will cling strongly to the guidance given by the spiritually enlightened. They are the key to building strong communities. Those who have reached enlightenment reflect the need to confront hypocrisy and dishonesty in order to promote truth and reality. They will uphold truth, justice, and respect.

Fifty-Fifth Letter – Favor

Favor bestowed here,
Yet the hereafter reigns vast,
In ranks and blessings.

We acknowledge that we have received many blessings. This applies to all sorts of individuals, communities, and nations. These blessings could include material wealth, status, talents, or other forms of prosperity.

However, despite the apparent differences in favor of individuals in this life, the true blessings and rewards await us in the hereafter. In the grand scheme of things, the hereafter holds greater significance in terms of both rank and favor.

The true nature of wealth and success is fleeting. They are nothing compared to the everlasting and unmatched blessings promised after death. Those seeking purity will prioritize the hereafter and will not focus only on worldly gains.

Those who seek enlightenment should reflect on the fleeting nature of possessions and achievements. They strive for only that which is everlasting and stop at nothing short of the Divine Essence.

Fifty-Sixth Letter – On the Day

On the Day of Truth,
Each soul reaps what it has sown,
Justice prevails firm.

The true forms of divine justice and accountability are found in the hereafter. The Day of Judgement is a day devoid of uncertainty. On this day, all souls will be gathered together, and each soul will be justly compensated for its actions without any inequity.

All individuals, regardless of their worldly status or circumstances, will stand equally before the judgment of a higher power. Each person will be held responsible for their conduct, intentions, and decisions they made during their earthly life.

Those who seek purity carry in their hearts the ultimate responsibility awaiting them in the hereafter. They strive to lead a life characterized by righteousness, morality, and adherence to ethical values. They acknowledge that every action carries consequences subject to divine evaluation.

Those who seek to complete their purity contemplate their behavior and ensure their full alignment with moral and ethical teachings. They contribute positively to their communities. They work to develop their sense of accountability and mindfulness. They recognize the inevitable answerability to a higher authority for one's choices.

Those who seek enlightenment carry a profound belief in divine justice and accountability. They strive to offer solace to others so that their endeavors toward goodness will be duly rewarded. They also caution those who engage in wrongdoing, signaling that they will face repercussions for their actions in the hereafter.

Fifty-Seventh Letter – Keys

Keys to the unseen,
Known only by the Divine,
All is in His sight.

The Creator is omniscient and omnipotent. He alone has the keys to the unseen. He is aware of everything known and unknown to mankind. The Creator's knowledge encompasses all of creation, down to the tiniest detail. He knows even when a leaf falls. He keeps everything in a clear record.

Those who seek purity are cognizant of the depth of Divine knowledge and power. They cement their belief in that singular Higher Power who possesses unfathomable wisdom and is aware of all things, both seen and unseen.

Those who seek to complete their purity acknowledge the complexity and interconnectedness of the universe. They acknowledge the vastness of the natural world. They accept that there are countless phenomena that are all within the control of this higher power.

Humanity has made much material progress in uncovering the universe's mysteries. However, the enlightened remind us to acknowledge the limits of human understanding. It is nothing compared to the boundless knowledge of the Divine.

Those who seek enlightenment trust the wisdom and providence of the Divine Entity. They submit to His knowing every detail of their lives, which gives them comfort and reassurance. This is especially true during uncertainty or adversity. They affirm that nothing escapes His Knowledge and that everything is under His control.

The spiritually enlightened show us the importance of faith and humility. They guide us to recognize the Creator's knowledge and wisdom, affirming His supremacy over all of existence.

Fifty-Eighth Letter – Different Beliefs

Different beliefs held,
Respect for diverse worship,
Unity in peace.

The human soul exists to worship. No human can ever be devoid of devotion. Devotion inevitably morphs into worship. Those who are unaware pursue different objects of devotion and worship. Different methods of devotion have morphed into different faiths.

This passage addresses the rejection of false beliefs. It emphasizes the distinction between different faiths. Humans are often devoted to someone or something. Their devotions become their object of worship. The Divine instructs humans to renounce idols. Those who reject this message of One True Divine Entity worship idols.

Adherents of the path embrace monotheism. They do not worship the same deities as others. They also do not engage in practices that contradict their belief in one supreme being. Instead, they are dedicated to worshiping the only One worthy of worship: the Creator.

Fifty-Ninth Letter – His Staff

His staff is in flight,
It swallows deceit with might,
Truth conquers the night.

Those who sincerely walk the path seeking enlightenment travel a journey of witnessing wonders. These wonders are secrets and mysteries of creation that the Divine reveals to those who befriend Him. Evil and misguidance can never hope to reveal any wonders of the mysteries of the Divine's creation. Instead, they try to imitate those wonders and trap those who walk the paths of darkness.

The story of one chosen servant of the Divine was that he manifested a miracle as a sign of the truth of his message. The people who followed misguidance attempted to use visual trickery to imitate that miracle in order to refute his claim. Instead, his miracle from the Divine trounced their efforts, and they were left dumbfounded.

Similarly, those who engage in a search for truth will find light and wisdom from the Divine as well as deceit from those who call away from the Divine's path. The truth and wisdom that the Divine reveals on His path will always outweigh misguidance.

Sixtieth Letter – Land Bears

Land bears witness true,
Solemn oath sworn to its soil,
Testimony pure.

Those who have reached enlightenment are given an intimate awareness of the physical universe. Every object, living and unliving, extolls the qualities of the Divine Entity. The enlightened can hear His praise reverberate through the cosmos. This praise also includes the testimony of the material world as to the existence of the Creator, the Oneness of that Creator, and the truth of His message. Every act we commit has witnesses. This testimony reflects the depth of this reality and the seriousness with which the Creator's chosen servants conducted themselves. It stresses that the teachings and principles these messengers brought are of utmost importance to human society.

Those who seek purity and enlightenment will strive to emulate the qualities of these chosen servants. They will seek to uphold righteousness and justice in any locale. They will demonstrate proper responsibility when living in any community. They attune their inner selves with the testimony echoed through the universe.

Sixty-First Letter – Fire

"O fire," We Said,
"Be coolness, safety for him."
Divine Mercy poured.

The spiritually enlightened remind us that the mercy and assistance of the Divine flow copiously upon those who stand firm on the truth. This is especially true when they do so in the face of adversity. Those who seek enlightenment inculcate the resilience to keep their principles in times of hardship. They understand that Divine help always comes in times of need.

The enlightened encourage us to develop trust in the Divine Entity. This trust can only be complete when one faces seemingly insurmountable challenges. When this trust reaches its zenith, we can overcome any obstacle.

Sixty-Second Letter – Messenger Arrives

Messenger arrives,
Compassionate, merciful,
Eases suffering.

The chosen servants of the Divine genuinely care about others. The suffering of others deeply distresses them. They seek to remedy this suffering by extending genuine compassion toward them. They are fully aware of the states of their communities. They know their trials and tribulations. Their kindness and gentle demeanor show their role as examples of compassion and mercy. They exhibit the virtues of kindness and benevolence toward all those they interact with. They personify these virtues the most through their roles as messengers and mentors. The compassionate soul of the mentor feels profound sorrow at the notion of anyone in his care descending into despair. He carefully oversees their journeys. Whenever one manifests belief, the mentor's compassion and mercy descend upon them. This manifestation and subsequent descent of the mentor's qualities mark the celebration of a great spiritual awakening.

Sixty-Third Letter – Messengers Walk

Messengers walk earth,
Eating, trading like us all,
Tests in patience, faith.

The spiritually enlightened teach us that the Divine's chosen servants are very special human beings. Though they are completely obedient to the Divine, they have their own feelings and will. They engage in the same activities we engage in. The beauty of Divine wisdom is that the Divine conveys it in a manner that is easy to learn and understand. His servants and friends are embodiments of the path so that everyone else can learn from them through observation and emulation. The path, its tenets, and its activities are never away from human activity. Rather, the path shows us what to do when one encounters difficulty during the course of normal life. The Divine has conveyed to us recommendations and examples of what to do and what not to do. His servants and friends serve as embodiments of those virtues and provide a clear picture of what enlightenment looks like. The path to the Divine does not take one away from normal life. Rather, it leads one through normal life to His presence.

Sixty-Fourth Letter – Claim

Or if we had claimed,
"We'd be better guided thus,"
Now clarity reigns.

The enlightened espouse timeless moral and ethical guidance. This guidance finds its origin in the teachings of the previous messengers, those who provided awareness of the Divine Entity. It allows people to navigate moral complexities. It helps them make ethical choices amidst changing times. Such guidance is essential, as it elevates a person into awareness of the unseen, the everlasting, and the eternal. Following true guidance and teachings fosters personal growth and character development. It also fosters community cohesion by stressing cooperation and compassion. It also provides spiritual fulfillment by illuminating a path to enlightenment and witnessing the Divine Essence. It helps humans uphold social justice, environmental stewardship, and human rights. Most importantly, it allows the actions of humankind to find permanence beyond this temporary world. It provides clarity amidst the impermanence of this life that clouds our collective judgment.

The enlightened teach us that clarity fully blossoms when the life of this world draws to a close. The guidance provided by the chosen servants of the Divine allows us to appreciate that clarity before our time on this Earth comes to an end.

Sixty-Fifth Letter – Respite

Respite I grant them,
Yet my plan stands resolute,
Firm in its design.

The enlightened seek to convey truth and reality to all souls. However, there are those who, after receiving truth and reality, regress into obstinate denial. The enlightened advise these people about the inevitability of Divine judgment. It will lead them to their deserved consequences in a way that surpasses their comprehension. The spiritually enlightened remind others of the Creator's sovereignty and justice. No one can feign ignorance after receiving their guidance. The enlightened emphasize that those who deny truth and reality will face repercussions, even if they claim to be unaware.

Sixty-Sixth Letter – Sent

They were sent to hear,
What their Lord revealed for them,
Warn their kin with haste.

The messengers of the Divine elucidate the attributes of those who follow the truth. Such people are resolute in their beliefs. They also show compassion toward others. Devoted to their worship, they seek blessings from the Divine and strive for the best. Their commitment is evident in their demeanor, marked by the signs of their devotion. References to them in previous passages underline their significance and ultimate triumph. The Divine promises them forgiveness for their missteps and great honor.

Sixty-Seventh Letter – Envious

Envious of Grace,
The Friend's kin, blessed with guidance,
Wisdom, mighty realm.

Is it wise to covet the blessings bestowed by the Divine upon others? Jealousy and ingratitude yield no benefit in any aspect of life. The Divine bestows wisdom and sovereignty upon whomever He chooses. We have no right to question or object to this divine decision. The Divine bestows special favors. So, it is crucial for us to always acknowledge and appreciate them.

Sixty-Eighth Letter – Weak

Weak, sick, or with naught,
No blame, if true to the path,
Righteousness prevails.

The enlightened do not attach value to physical capability alone. They offer reassurance and compassion to everyone, especially for those facing hardships, such as the weak, the sick, or the poor. These people are free of blame for their inability to materially contribute to society as long as they are sincere in their devotion to the Divine. Furthermore, the enlightened do not judge or penalize others for their misdeeds as long as they continue to strive to uphold virtue within themselves. The enlightened forever espouse forgiveness and mercy. The foundation of enlightenment is the understanding of human limits and the Divine's limitless compassion for His servants.

Sixty-Ninth Letter – Foreign Lands

If to foreign lands,
Our message were revealed,
Paths of faith unfold.

Leaders face unique struggles when conveying a message to their people amidst opposition. Without Divine assistance, the opposing forces might have influenced the leader, if only a little. The enlightened tell us that the Divine acknowledges this struggle. They underscore the importance of Divine assistance and guidance in the face of adversity. The Divine is aware of the vulnerability of even the most steadfast people when faced with opposition and hardship. The enlightened remind us of human nature and dependence on Divine help in conveying the truth.

Seventieth Letter – Lord's Mark

Lord's mark, excess shown,
Divine judgment, clear signal,
Heed the warning call.

The enlightened teach that those who oppose truth and reality still have the opportunity to accept guidance until their last breath. However, they will have no chance to turn back after this life ends. On the Day of Judgment, those who espoused truth and reality will turn away from those who rejected truth and persisted in their denial. Once the trumpet that heralds the Day of Judgment blasts, people will be called to face the results of their deeds.

Even in this life, those who seek purity detach themselves from those who persistently reject the truth. The enlightened encourage others to focus on their own virtue and devotion. Those who seek to complete their purity are unswayed by the disbelief or misguidance of others.

Those who seek enlightenment are concerned first and foremost with the reality of their own judgment. For them, every day is a new form of submission and a reminder to heed the call of Judgment Day.

Seventy-First Letter – Names

*"Call Him the Divine
or call Him the Merciful,
Best names are for Him.*

*In prayer, restraint,
Be neither loud nor silent,
You should be balanced."*

The enlightened remind us to constantly turn to the Divine for His mercy, help, and guidance. They guide us to the rich world of divine attributes and teach others to approach it with sincerity. Those who seek purity invoke those divine qualities that resonate with their needs. They also maintain a balanced and respectful demeanor during devotion and adopt a moderate and mindful approach to worship. In this way, they traverse the world of divine attributes and reach the divine essence.

Seventy-Second Letter – Mockers

Mockers claim falsehood,
"If I forged it," retort made,
Their crimes, not Mine, laid.

The enlightened teach that life is a continuous test. Everyone faces trials in many forms. These trials are a reflection of the choices a human being must make in this life. The choice to follow guidance for a community or society is often embodied in one person. This person is a locus of divine attention and mercy. The spiritually deficient will seek to dismiss that individual by attributing claims of falsehood and forgery to him. However, people who earnestly pursue righteousness and truth will naturally take guidance from that individual and rely less on others. Their purity finds completion. They find sufficiency in the Divine Entity alone.

Seventy-Third Letter – Heed

Heed the Divine's words,
Messenger's duty, clear path,
Turn away, beware.

The enlightened urge people to avoid intoxicants, gambling, idol worship, and superstition. They emphasize that these behaviors are spiritually harmful and attributed to evil. By avoiding these vices, people can easily attain purity.

Conversely, engaging in these activities enhances spiritual decline. The signs of this decline are found in both individuals and society. Those who seek purity avoid such behaviors through their commitment to constant submission. This protects them from spiritual harm.

Submission is the bedrock of guidance provided by the Divine. This guidance pervades all parts of their lives. It guarantees spiritual well-being in this life and the hereafter.

Seventy-Fourth Letter – One House

In them, only one
House of steadfast Believers,
Unity's stronghold.

In ancient Egypt, a common person rose against a powerful ruler. Despite the ruler having a huge majority of followers, only one family shared the common citizen's beliefs and values.

This family was a tiny minority in a sea of obstinate denial. They are a small but important example of people who dared to think deeply, even when surrounded by a civilization that rejected guidance. This historical reference reminds us that, even when facing much opposition, people have always dared to question inconsistent beliefs. It shows the importance of critical thinking, conviction, and the power of minority perspectives. When truth and reality permeate the heart, that heart becomes a stronghold against multitudes.

Seventy-Fifth Letter – Fleeting

Life's fleeting journey,
Return to innocence lost,
His wisdom prevails.

The Creator has endowed humanity with certain faculties. Human birth itself is miraculous in nature. This birth signifies the Divine's power and care in bringing humans into the world. Humans have three key faculties: hearing, vision, and intellect. They let people perceive and understand the world around them. Despite these faculties, humans enter this world in an initial state of ignorance. They have an inevitable need for guidance. Humans must use the resources they have to recognize blessings and give thanks for guidance and provision. The enlightened appreciate the gift of life. They are those who develop their abilities in the light of the guidance they receive. They forever show gratitude to the Source.

Seventy-Sixth Letter – Earth's Heirs

If We desired,
Angels could have been Earth's heirs,
Divine will prevails.

The enlightened are those who are in awe of the Divine's absolute power and authority. They are aware that the Creator has the power to appoint angels as rulers over humans. Instead of humans, they could have been directing people's affairs. However, the Divine chose humans to be His representatives and leaders on Earth. This shows the significance of human responsibility and agency. It also reflects the ineffable wisdom of the Divine. In essence, humans have been given a huge trust and duty. They are responsible for leading and caring for the Earth. This responsibility prompts reflection on our actions and decisions.

Seventy-Seventh Letter – Work

"Work to your limits,"
Prophet says, shows example,
Righteousness prevails.

Enlightened leaders are fully committed to their duties. They serve as exemplars for their communities. They enjoin hard work upon their constituents, emphasizing that the consequences of actions will become clear in the future. Those who do good deeds will ultimately achieve a positive outcome. The message is simple: people should own their actions and fulfill their duties. This is why the enlightened stress the importance of accountability and responsibility. Our choices have repercussions, serving as a reminder that we will be judged based on our deeds. Those who seek enlightenment strive to be mindful of their actions. They become cognizant of accountability and responsibility in all parts of life. They recognize the importance of all of our decisions in shaping our final outcome.

Seventy-Eighth Letter – Honest Hearts

Honest hearts find honor,
Hypocrites face judgment's call,
Mercy may pardon.

The enlightened constantly remind us of the importance of sincerity and faithfulness. The Divine promises honor for those who stay sincere in their beliefs and adhere to His path. He has also warned of disgrace for hypocrites. They are those who pretend to believe while harboring disloyalty. However, the Divine will also show mercy and forgiveness to those who sincerely repent and change. In essence, the enlightened are those who urge and value honesty and authenticity. They do not tolerate hypocrisy and insincerity. They seek forgiveness and mercy when they fall short, trusting in the Divine's compassion and grace. Those who seek purity first think deeply about their intentions and actions. They strive for truth, forgiveness, and mercy.

Seventy-Ninth Letter – Belief

Belief guides actions,
Honor earned with grace bestowed,
Pride brings torment near.

The Divine interacts with a human being primarily through one's level of gratitude. If they are grateful for the blessings they have, the Divine honors them to the point where He grants them even more blessings. However, ungratefulness eventually leads to spiritual decay and disgrace. The reality is that gratitude itself, as well as accountability, are two very important tools for assessing one's relationship with the Divine. In essence, they serve as benchmarks to measure one's spiritual strength. The results of gratitude are manifestations of the Creator's benevolence. The spiritually enlightened use these results to acknowledge and appreciate His blessings in their lives. Those who seek purity give themselves to trust in the Divine's justice and mercy. The purity they gain helps foster gratitude and appreciation in all aspects of life.

Eightieth Letter – In the Land

In the land you'll stay,
For those who fear, heed, obey
Divine decree guides.

Spiritual enlightenment comes with a sense of stability and permanence. This is the true manner in which the Divine Entity establishes His creatures in the land. Stability is to be constantly aware of the Divine's majesty, which includes His power, authority, and wisdom. Permanence lies in acknowledging the results of disobedience. It is to recognize the Divine's warning signs and take them seriously. Those who seek purity learn to recognize true stability. Those who seek wisdom are conscious of the Divine's authority and heed His warnings. Those who seek enlightenment learn to align themselves with His infinite wisdom. Those who seek guidance inculcate humility, accountability, and obedience before the Creator.

Eighty-First Letter – Their Lord

Their Lord replied thus:
No toil shall be wasted here,
Equal in His sight.

The human soul comes from an origin that is neither male nor female. All those who endeavor to return to the source are equally recognized for their efforts. There are those who have endured forced migration, expulsion from their homes, and persecution for their beliefs, all in devotion to the Source. There are even some who have given their lives. The Divine holds all such souls in high regard for their choices, regardless of gender or status. Similarly, the spiritually enlightened value and respect everyone's contributions. They remind others to remain true to the source and to support each other in hard times.

Eighty-Second Letter – Creation's Purpose

Creation's purpose,
Not in vain, disbelief's ploy,
Woe to those who doubt.

Those who seek enlightenment reflect on the purpose and meaning behind the Divine's creative act. They become privy to the secrets of the universe, knowing that the Divine originated all that is known and all that is yet unknown. They acknowledge a divine plan and intention behind it all. The spiritually deficient assume the universe and life as lacking purpose or meaning. Therefore, they come to deny the existence of the Creator. The enlightened warn of dire consequences for those who become obstinate in that denial. They caution that disbelief leads to disgrace in the hereafter. They remind us to reflect upon our own existence. They urge us to appreciate the beauty and complexity of the universe as manifestations of the Divine's wisdom. Also, they urge us to think about the results of disbelief. Those results appear in one's quality of life as well as the hereafter. True conviction leads to action, and each action carries one's honor or disgrace.

Eighty-Third Letter – Gathered

Gathered by the Lord,
Wise, Knowing, His decree firm,
All shall meet their fate.

The enlightened accept the Divine's role as the ultimate gatherer of humanity. They emphasize that He will bring all individuals together for judgment and accountability, regardless of their beliefs, actions, or status. They highlight the Divine's attributes of wisdom and knowledge. They affirm His control over all of creation. They remind others of His wisdom and knowledge in guiding the course of events. They underscore the inevitability of being gathered and facing reckoning before the Creator. Those who seek enlightenment work to recognize the Divine's Sovereignty in all aspects of life. They strive to trust Him even in uncertain times. They concern themselves with preparing for that ultimate reckoning and judgment by living a life of virtue. Trust in the Divine and confidence in His wisdom are the stepping stones to enlightenment.

Eighty-Fourth Letter – Reward

The Divine has bequeathed several positive affinities to the human soul. These affinities include the natural gravitation to justice and honor. Indeed, the Divine accords honor to those who make honorable choices. Furthermore, this honor that the Divine bestows is not random. It exceeds the bounds of mere equitability, showcasing the Divine's wisdom and grace. The enlightened pull back the veils of this universe and reveal the Creator's role as a bestower of honor. Honor is a result of choosing an honorable path. The enlightened explain honor in part as the appreciation of the Creator's blessings and grace. Ultimately, it is the culmination of trust in the Divine's kindness. Those who seek purity begin by seeking out the path to His honor.

Eighty-Fifth Letter – Messengers Convey

Messengers convey
Glad tidings and warnings clear,
No excuse remains.

The virtue of divine guidance is that it is complete. The Creator selected messengers to convey the intricacies of His guidance to His creatures. In this manner, they made certain that no ambiguity remains. The objective of divine guidance is the complete elimination of ignorance. The messengers aimed to ensure that humanity had complete awareness of the Creator's existence. With the delivery of their message, the responsibility to follow their path falls to individuals. Each human has the choice of heeding the message and aligning their actions accordingly. The enlightened teach us this truth and highlight the Divine's omnipotence and wisdom. They emphasize His role of providing guidance and subsequently judging humanity. Those who seek enlightenment must seek out guidance from the wellsprings of wisdom that the Divine has placed in the hearts of His chosen servants. They must take ownership of their beliefs and actions and acknowledge the Divine's sovereignty and wisdom in all matters. Those who complete their purity acknowledge the Divine's servants and the warnings they provide. By valuing prophetic guidance, acting responsibly, and recognizing the Divine's authority and wisdom, they strive for greater spiritual heights.

Eighty-Sixth Letter – Do People Assume?

Do people assume
Belief without trials endured?
Tests forge true faith's fire.

Conviction cannot be proven without putting it to the test. When a person completes various tests of that conviction, they reach the stages of enlightenment. Mere declarations of faith do not exempt one from life's challenges. Conviction does not come about without resilience and action. Conviction in truth and reality undergoes refinement and enhancement through trials. The trials of life serve as reminders that genuine belief requires perseverance amidst adversity. Those who seek enlightenment strive to move beyond superficial declarations of faith. They recognize challenges as opportunities for spiritual growth. They constantly renew their commitment to living out their beliefs through action.

Eighty-Seventh Letter – Ask

Ask, what to bestow?
Charity for all in need,
Divine sees every deed.

Those who seek purity seek to purify even their wealth and resources. One of their primary concerns regarding their wealth is how best to spend it. The enlightened encourage selflessness. Charity is a requirement of the path. They instruct that charity begins with those closest to you, starting with one's own family. It extends further to relatives, orphans, the impoverished, and travelers in need. Every act a person does privately or publicly is observed and noted in the sight of the Divine. For the enlightened, the true outcome of selflessness is the Divine's special attention.

Eighty-Eighth Letter – To Resolve

To resolve disputes,
Unveiling truth and falsehood,
Guidance for the lost.

The spiritually enlightened are not free of disputes and disagreements in life. Rather, they seek to resolve their disputes in the light of Divine guidance. The Creator acknowledges disputation among humanity, speaking at length on a range of topics. These include theological concepts, existential questions, and interpretations of prophetic teachings. Divine guidance also serves to unmask fallacies and deceptions that false disputation seeks to propagate. The Creator has provided a clear message in order to provide clarity amidst divergent views. Those who reach enlightenment take this message wholeheartedly. They become the means by which individuals take guidance toward truth and understanding. Divine guidance has also provided instruction on how to deal with disputation. The spiritually enlightened seek resolution through open dialogue. They strive for intellectual and spiritual honesty. Ultimately, the path of enlightenment is to embrace the pursuit of truth and clarity.

Eighty-Ninth Letter – Blessed

Blessed yet selfish,
Withholding what's been given.
Touched by good, unkind.

The spiritually deficient are not without favorable circumstances or blessings. Rather, they react to these blessings by behaving selfishly and miserly. The enlightened shun this behavior. Those who seek enlightenment strive to exemplify generosity and gratitude. They become aware of the pitfalls of selfishness and ingratitude. Enlightenment lies in the appreciation of blessings and sharing them with others. Those who seek purity will use what they have to benefit themselves as well as others. Those who seek enlightenment strive for new heights of selflessness. Those who reach enlightenment become paragons of generosity for others.

Ninetieth Letter – Yearning

Yearning for old ways,
Ignorance's dark grasp they seek.
God's judgment surpass.

Divine guidance gives a clear demarcation between those who seek enlightenment and those who remain obstinate in their spiritual deficiency. The spiritually deficient have an aversion to Divine guidance. This is reflected in their yearning to follow practices and rituals that have no connection to the Divine's message. Moving against Divine guidance is cause for chaos and injustice. The enlightened acknowledge that the Divine's wisdom and justice are superior to every other standard. Those who seek purity strive for true conviction in the Divine's guidance and principles. The path to enlightenment begins with critiquing the inclination to reject Divine guidance. Those who follow it embrace trust in the Divine's wisdom. The spiritually enlightened strive for moral and spiritual clarity. The spiritually deficient remain mired in regressive ideologies that lead to arrogance and obstinacy.

Ninety-First Letter – Nights

Ten solemn nights pass
Significant, yet concise,
Their meaning sacred.

The spiritually enlightened never take any single day for granted. They are cognizant of the reality that every day is a new day. Indeed, certain days and nights hold special significance in terms of the Divine's bestowal of blessings. Those who seek purity seek out these days and engage in remembrance of the Creator, seeking His special mercy. Those who seek enlightenment use these days as opportunities for spiritual reflection and renewal. The nobility of enlightenment settles in the heart when seekers utilize these sacred moments to deepen their connection with the Divine.

Ninety-Second Letter – People of the Woods

People of the Woods,
In their wrongdoing, strayed far,
Seeking paths astray.

The path of enlightenment requires an undeviating direction. If one's spiritual compass is off by a single degree, the direction of one's spiritual travel will miss the mark. "People of the Woods" refers to an ancient Arabian tribe known for their residence in wooded areas. "Wrongdoing" denotes their unjust, oppressive, and rebellious behavior against the Divine's commands. Their ways began as pure, but they later added injustices to their culture. Their deviance caused them to stray far from the path of enlightenment. People of the past who deviated in this way received guidance from the Divine through His chosen servants. However, those who rejected that guidance ultimately met with destruction. This is the final destination of spiritual deficiency.

Ninety-Third Letter – Clear Signs

He brought them clear signs,
yet doubt still reigned in their hearts.
God guides the skeptic.

The Divine's chosen messengers bring clear signs and guidance to their people. Despite the undeniable clarity of these signs, the spiritually deficient cling stubbornly to their doubt and disbelief. Their obstinacy endures such that when a messenger leaves them, they pretend as if they never received guidance. Their pretense reflects a glaring lack of understanding. It is indicative of arrogance and presumption. These qualities persist in an unhealthy skepticism that corrupts their hearts. In this manner, they stray further and further from truth and reality. The enlightened can offer nothing to such people except admonishment and warnings against arrogance and presumptive skepticism. However, if such people heed these warnings, the seeds of enlightenment can still take root in their hearts. Individuals will always have the choice to embrace truth and avoid the path of persistent doubt and disbelief.

Ninety-Fourth Letter – In that Place

Gathered in that place,
All, distant ones brought near now,
Answer for deeds done.

Humanity will be gathered in one place to face the judgment of the One. That one place is the plain of resurrection on that solemn day. The Divine's inclusive judgment will bring even those who did not accept it in life near. All are summoned before Him to face the consequences of their actions. The Divine's judgment is comprehensive. The enlightened remind others of this universal scope—both for mercy and for justice. They urge individuals to embrace their responsibility and seek virtue in anticipation of the Day of Judgement.

Ninety-Fifth Letter – Enter

"Enter into Hell,
to abide eternally."
Wretched end for pride.

Enlightenment involves the removal of veils. These veils conceal the realities of creation. Ultimately, they are barriers between the Divine and humankind. The first veils that a seeker removes are the veils of deficient character traits. Among the most spiritually deficient of these traits is pride. Pride is something that the Divine has promised a wretched end for. It is the trait that sums up obstinate denial of truth and reality. Someone who works to remove pride from the heart will eventually witness the realities surrounding the Divine's commandments. This can be the case even if that person struggles with other deficient character traits. However, if a person works to inculcate good character in themselves, pride can still hinder them from the Divine light. Those who stubbornly cling to pride will face permanent repercussions in the hereafter. Just as they are barred from the Divine light in this life, they will face an existence barred from it in the next. Those who strive for enlightenment seek humility before the Divine, adherence to His guidance, and avoidance of extreme hubris that leads to corruption of the heart.

Ninety-Sixth Letter – Messengers Consume

Messengers, consume
Goodness, integrity shines
Divine sees your deeds

The enlightened teach the way of the Divine's chosen messengers. Their past consists of physical and spiritual enrichment. To achieve this, they consume only what is wholesome – whether it be nourishment, knowledge, or general positivity that uplifts body and spirit. Furthermore, they conduct themselves with honesty, transparency, and intense integrity in all of their interactions and endeavors. They live life completely cognizant of their inherent accountability for their actions. Most importantly, they constantly acknowledge the Creator's intimate awareness of their thoughts, words, and deeds. These messengers passed this way down to their followers, who attained enlightenment by adhering to their teachings. After the messengers, the friends of the Divine embraced the responsibility of conveying the Divine's message. These friends are the spiritually enlightened. They encourage others to similarly cultivate awareness of the Divine and lead by example.

Ninety-Seventh Letter – Proof

Proof from your Lord shines,
Clear light guides through darkened paths,
Divine truth revealed

The Divine light is that timeless modality by which seekers find guidance, clarity, purity, and illumination. The enlightened teach us that guidance is to acknowledge the Divine's existence and the message He revealed to humanity. Clarity is to deepen one's understanding and appreciation of the Divine after reflection on the Divine's signs in creation. Purity is to overcome life's challenges using the teachings established by Divine guidance. Illumination is the inescapable awareness of His Essence. When seekers progress through these stages, sharing the light of Divine wisdom becomes a natural outcome. When one reaches the stages of enlightenment, one spreads the message of Divine truths to inspire and guide those around them. Cultivating awareness of the Divine's presence and wisdom will always strengthen one's spirituality. It opens the doors of the heart, allowing the clear light of guidance to nourish the soul.

Ninety-Eighth Letter – A Day

A Day promised near,
Time's flow unchecked, fate defined,
In its grasp we're held.

The spiritually enlightened recognize the finite nature of time and prioritize actions accordingly. Those who strive for enlightenment embrace the present moment. Dwelling on the past or worrying about the future only detracts from opportunities in the present. With the Day of Judgement firmly etched into their hearts, procrastination loses its appeal. They realize that time cannot be delayed or extended. Furthermore, the accountability inherently linked to Judgement Day prompts a mindful approach to decision-making and behavior. The spiritually enlightened express appreciation for life's blessings. They cultivate in others gratitude for the time allotted to them. Through this approach, seekers find life's purpose and live purposely.

Ninety-Ninth Letter – Luxury

Luxury abounds,
Spouses as beautiful stars,
Paradise's bliss.

The way of enlightenment requires focus on this life as well as the hereafter. Those who seek enlightenment learn to appreciate the good things they enjoy in their present lives. They develop a strong sense of gratitude for whatever they experience from the Divine Entity. They find strength by seeking tranquility in the heart. This means that they learn to find contentment in their connection with the Divine. Additionally, they cherish relationships with their loved ones and value the beauty of companionship. Those who seek purity strive for spiritual refinement and self-improvement through the purification of the heart and soul. They eventually come to live with intention and purpose. For such individuals, these qualities represent a life of comfort and fulfillment. The spiritually enlightened advise others that true solace and comfort come from the Creator. As such, they encourage others to seek refuge in their relationship with Him. Ultimately, the enlightened teach us to strive for the realm of permanent bliss, where everlasting comfort and joy await those who walk the path with purity and determination.

One Hundredth Letter – My Lord Provides

My Lord provides all,
His bounty endless, assured,
Spend, replaced by Him.

The spiritually enlightened spend in the way of the Divine, knowing that He replaces everything spent. Those who seek enlightenment learn to trust the process of the Divine's provision regardless of their financial circumstances. Gratitude becomes paramount as they grow in appreciation for the blessings for what they have. They inculcate contentment in every situation. In keeping with these truths, the enlightened encourage giving generously for the sake of the Divine. Furthermore, they encourage others to live within their means and avoid excessive spending and debt. Individuals who follow this advice come to the understanding that true provision comes from the Creator alone. They also advise others to develop detachment from material attractions, as material wealth is ultimately transient and temporary. Those who seek purity look to Divine guidance to manage their resources in the best manner. Embracing these truths bolsters one's connection to and relationship with the Divine. It inculcates a sense of deep trust, gratitude, and contentment. These qualities comprise the purity that one needs in order to share wealth with others, lead balanced financial lives, and find peace and security in the Divine's provision.

One Hundred First Letter – Ancient Paths

Ancient paths faded,
Unbelief persists, despite,
Wisdom lost in time.

Enlightenment is not limited to a particular time period or outlook. Those who walk the path of enlightenment draw lessons from history. They draw wisdom and insight from the experiences and mistakes of previous generations. In doing so, they strive to avoid the mistakes of their predecessors. They embrace flexibility in their daily affairs. In these matters, seeking guidance from Divine teachings becomes essential. Divine guidance serves as a timeless source of wisdom and truth for navigating life's complexities. Those who seek enlightenment learn to be mindful of the cultural and societal influences that shape their views and actions. They strive to rise above shortsightedness and bias. They eventually cultivate a critical and discerning mindset. They question empty assumptions and instead seek deep knowledge and understanding. Those who reach enlightenment focus on the present moment and plan flexibly for the future. Their understanding of previous civilizations and cultures is informed by their relationship of trust and conviction in the Divine Entity.

One Hundred Second Letter – One Being

One Being supreme,
Denying hearts, arrogance,
Hereafter ignored.

The spiritually enlightened are those who acknowledge the Divine Entity with the totality of their beings. They affirm the Oneness of the Divine. They acknowledge Him as the sole Creator and Sustainer of all existence. They affirm belief in the hereafter, recognizing the Day of Judgement and the everlasting consequences of their actions. In keeping with these truths, they embrace humility, understanding their place among creation and their reliance on the Divine's mercy. They caution against arrogance, teaching that it blinds individuals to the truth and wisdom inherent in the Divine's guidance. They cultivate compassion and empathy toward those with differing beliefs in themselves and others. In doing so, they help to foster understanding and mutual respect. They share the teachings of the Divine's messengers with forbearance and compassion, allowing others to explore the beauty and wisdom of these teachings. They live with purpose and a sense of accountability in anticipation of the hereafter. Thus, they inspire others to lead righteous and meaningful lives. Those who follow the spiritually enlightened learn to deepen their connection with the Divine by embracing all of these qualities. They strive for purity, leading balanced and fulfilling lives in the process. As their spiritual aspirations become higher, they nurture a strong sense of conviction, compassion, and purpose.

One Hundred Third Letter – Guests

The Friend's guests arrived,
Honorable, story told,
Lessons in their stay.

The enlightened draw lessons from the stories of the Divine's chosen servants. In the story of the chosen friend who was visited by three angels, the first lesson they draw is of hospitality. The chosen servant exemplified a welcoming and hospitable nature toward his guests. Individuals can apply these qualities of being a good host by extending warmth and hospitality to guests in their own homes. The second lesson they derive is one of respect. The chosen servant demonstrated this by behaving humbly toward his guests. Individuals can emulate this respect by behaving humbly with others, regardless of their background or status. The third lesson is generosity. The chosen servant offered food to his guests, even though they were strangers. By being generous and kind toward others, individuals can cultivate a spirit of goodwill and compassion in their interactions. The fourth lesson is patience. The chosen servant waited for his guests to eat and rest before inquiring about their purpose. Similarly, individuals can practice patience and refrain from rushing to conclusions in their interactions with others. The fifth lesson is open-mindedness. The chosen servant was willing to listen to his guests despite them being strangers. By being open-minded and receptive to different perspectives, individuals can foster understanding and mutual respect in their relationships. The final major lesson is the importance of gratitude. The chosen servant in this example expressed gratitude for the blessings of the Divine after hearing from his guests. Overall, by reflecting on this story and its lessons, individuals can strive to lead more virtuous and fulfilling lives.

One Hundred Fourth Letter – Resting

Resting by the rock,
Fish forgotten, devil's trick,
River finds its way.

Those who seek purity learn to gain awareness of their spiritual enemies. The most blatant of these enemies is the devil. Purity requires one to be vigilant against his whispers and temptations. The second enemy is the ego, which seeks to deflect blame from itself. This is reflected in the story of two travelers seeking to meet a messenger of the Divine. The second companion was carrying a fish for their food, but it escaped his grasp, and he forgot to mention it. Instead of deflecting blame, the companion acknowledges his mistake of forgetting the fish. Those who seek purity work constantly to emulate this example. They strive to maintain mindfulness in both thought and action. In order to remain present and focused on their goals and values, they seek support and guidance from the Divine. Those who seek to complete their purity draw wisdom from Divine guidance when faced with challenges and difficulties. Those who seek enlightenment cultivate self-awareness by understanding their strengths and weaknesses. They learn that the key to self-improvement lies in the power of forgiveness toward both oneself and others. They view mistakes as opportunities for growth and learning. The spiritually enlightened are those who draw inspiration from the examples given by the Divine. They, in turn, become examples themselves to guide others.

Part Two:

REALITY

Many search for Him, but few truly seek Him.

- Waqar Faiz

One Hundred Fifth Letter – Maturity

Maturity reached,
Wisdom and knowledge bestowed,
Reward for the just.

The journey of each enlightened soul parallels the journey of every human being. Those who reach enlightenment know full well that each of us can grow and develop skills. Each of us is capable of making smart decisions. Arm yourself with wisdom and insight. They will help you overcome life's obstacles. Those who attain purity pursue success with hard work. This leads to realizing our goals and gaining recognition for our efforts. The enlightened inspire us to use our full potential. They are exemplars of exercising good judgment and the pursuit of excellence. Their way applies to all parts of life. These examples are still invaluable in today's world.

One Hundred Sixth Letter – Horses

Glistening horses,
Are shown in evening light,
Beauty enchants him.

As you move further along your spiritual journey, you will start to see that your free will is far deeper than simply making decisions. It becomes a profound examination of character, humility, and fidelity to higher principles. The chosen servants of the Divine do not make hasty decisions based only on personal understanding. Instead, they turn to the Divine for guidance.

Horses are manifestations of remarkable tranquility and poise while still. They are also manifestations of astonishing swiftness and agility when in motion. Such beauty is enough to capture the attention of even a close chosen servant of the Divine. However, those who have reached enlightenment do not remain lost in this beauty. They understand that this beauty of creation is but a small ember compared to the bonfire of divine beauty. They certainly appreciate what the Divine has created. Nevertheless, they always pause and turn back to the Divine, ensuring that this beauty does not become a distraction for them.

We all grapple with moral dilemmas, so we must turn to higher principles for guidance. We must remember the virtues of humility, repentance, and reliance on divine wisdom. These virtues will help us navigate life's challenges.

One Hundred Seventh Letter – Cursed

Cursed in this life's span,
And on Judgment Day, dismay,
Their path leads to woe.

Consider a scenario. A community leader tries to steer his town away from corruption. He aims to lead it toward honest governance. Despite his persistent efforts, many in the town remain entrenched in their corrupt practices.

People dismiss and defy his attempts to reform. Instead of heeding his warnings, corrupt individuals challenge the leader. They ask him to prove his claims by causing the consequences he warns of.

Their challenge to him reflects their recalcitrance and unwillingness to acknowledge the truth. They do not admit wrongdoing, nor do they try to reform. Instead, they defiantly dare the guide to speed up the consequences he warns of. This response illustrates their stubbornness and lack of remorse for their actions.

In the end, the town faces the results of their corruption. Downturns and disasters rock the community. This serves as a reminder of the repercussions of arrogance, dishonesty, and defiance in the face of efforts for positive change.

We must ask ourselves if our attitudes are the same as the people in this scenario. Are we keeping open minds and hearts to grow in our spirituality, or are we steeping ourselves in negativity and skepticism? The answers to those questions will determine the course our lives will take.

One Hundred Eighth Letter – He Urged

He urged them to throw,
Illusions deceived the crowd,
Potent magic wrought.

The soul and the ego have different origins. As such, one often inclines toward truth and the other toward falsehood. In the struggle between truth and falsehood, those under the ego's sway use deceptive tactics to falsely show their own strength. They themselves are deceived, so they, in turn, deceive and mislead others.

For example, consider the following scenario. People use clever marketing to create illusions of superiority or effectiveness for their products or services. At first, these illusions seem real. However, consumers eventually discover the truth about what they are presented with.

In another example, some leaders or groups use lies or fear tactics. They do this to scare and control public opinion. However, with time and access to accurate information, the true nature of their deceit becomes apparent to the public.

The enlightened remind us of the transient nature of falsehood and the ultimate triumph of truth. They encourage critical thinking in the face of deception. Most importantly, awareness of the Divine Entity will allow one to apply honesty and integrity in all of life.

One Hundred Ninth Letter – Revealed

Divine's Word revealed,
Full of guidance and wisdom,
In revelations.

The basis of revealed guidance is rooted in wisdom. Wisdom is to comprehend the importance of clear understanding and good judgment. When life becomes confusing, understand the situation and then use that judgment to make the best choices. Similar to using a flashlight in the dark to see, use wisdom instead of just following the trends of society. Instilling wisdom within the heart is not difficult. Every day, make an effort to make choices that align with your principles. Look closely at the information you have. Examine its origin and make the best choices accordingly. This process enables us to develop the wisdom necessary to make choices that match our principles. It also encourages people from different backgrounds to understand each other better. Wisdom is a bridge that connects people with different destinations and ways. However, those who follow wisdom with sincerity will travel the path to its end.

One Hundred Tenth Letter – Wonder

In wonder she asked,
"How can I, untouched, bear one?"
A son, a marvel.

Life is a series of ups and downs. Those who seek purpose and peace should know that it cannot come in this life without turbulence. The key to moving past this turbulence is trust and submission. He has given us many examples of this in the lives of His servants and friends. One such friend received an extraordinary announcement from an angel. She became perplexed and amazed. However, the Divine bestows blessings, aid, purpose, and peace in ways that the mind often cannot comprehend. This example showcases unwavering trust and wholehearted surrender to the Divine. Despite her perplexity, she chose to trust the Divine's pronouncement, even when the "how" seemed impossible to comprehend.

Those who sincerely seek purpose can draw inspiration from this example. It inspires us to embrace the unknown with the knowledge that the Divine will provide assistance in His perfect timing. Let us follow this example and seek divine guidance and clarity. Let us seek from Him wisdom and understanding. Ultimately, let us surrender to the Divine's will. Let us trust that He acts in our best interests. Doing so will allow us to deepen our trust and faith, find strength in our beliefs, and navigate life's challenges with confidence.

One Hundred Eleventh Letter – Lord's Path

Towards my Lord's path,
Guidance sought; faith, no waver,
Journey with Divine.

Enlightenment is a journey of trust. Those who seek purity learn first to trust in Divine guidance. This translates to the conviction that the Divine will guide them through life's journey. Those who seek to complete their purity seek a close relationship with the Divine. They recognize Him in their hearts as their Ultimate Sovereign and seek to deepen their bond with Him. Those who seek enlightenment learn to adopt an optimistic and hopeful outlook. Their struggle is geared toward gnosis of the Divine Entity. Therefore, their trust in the Divine is that He will showcase new and deeper wisdoms through life's challenges and uncertainties. Eventually, they come to understand the importance of taking initiative with respect to their goals and aspirations. They take steps with the trust that the Creator will provide guidance to them along the way. As they move forward with the Creator's guidance, they inculcate increased self-reflection and introspection within themselves. Furthermore, they learn to embrace the unknown with confidence. They trust that divine guidance will lead them through uncertain times, even when the path is unclear. Those who reach enlightenment turn constantly to the Divine for support. Their journey of trust has given them total conviction that the Creator is always with them, providing guidance and protection. The spiritually enlightened guide others to the journey of trust, allowing them to find comfort and solace in the Divine Presence.

One Hundred Twelfth Letter – They Embarked

They embarked aboard,
Until, when the boat set sail,
He caused it to breach.

He questioned, "Did you
Intentionally damage?"
An act grave, indeed.

The spiritually enlightened often allude to the stories and parables provided in Divine guidance. One such story is that of two chosen servants of the Divine who embark upon a journey and board a ship. Upon disembarking, one of them intentionally damages the vessel, prompting the other to question his actions. The enlightened give us many different lessons from this story. The first is to appreciate what we possess, symbolized by the safety and security of the ship. The second is to avoid engaging in behavior harmful to oneself and others. Instead, those who seek purity must strive to make positive choices by reflecting on their actions and potential consequences. The third is to seek guidance and wisdom from those with more experience and knowledge. Those who seek enlightenment must remain open to learning and growth. The fourth is to engage in deep introspection. Those who seek enlightenment must regularly examine their thoughts, words, and deeds, making adjustments as needed. The fifth lesson is to embrace patience in the face of uncertainty or adversity. Those who reach enlightenment are the ones who have fully embraced these teachings. Their lessons become engraved onto their hearts as they prepare to meet their Creator.

One Hundred Thirteenth Letter
– They Rejected Him

They rejected him,
"Educated, but crazy!"
Dismissal's bitter.

Seeking knowledge and wisdom is no trivial pursuit. You must make a commitment to continuous learning. Those who actively seek out opportunities for deeper education and personal growth unlock their potential for becoming seekers of the Divine.

Those who wish to share their knowledge or ideas with others must also be prepared for the possibility of facing ridicule or criticism. The mark of enlightenment is the ability to stay grounded in one's beliefs and values. It is to maintain confidence in the validity of your perspective, even in the face of skepticism.

Becoming a true seeker requires cultivating your character instead of prioritizing outward appearances. Those who seek enlightenment dedicate themselves to developing virtues such as compassion, empathy, and integrity. They place greater importance on inner growth. Thus, they avoid seeking validation from unqualified sources.

Those who seek enlightenment avoid making judgments about others based solely on appearance or background. Seek to understand individuals on a deeper level. Learn to appreciate unique perspectives and contributions.

Finally, no one can become a true seeker without cultivating persistence and patience. Wise individuals often encounter resistance and rejection yet remain resilient in the face of adversity.

Maintain these commitments, and the path to true seeking will open up to you. Stay true to these principles, and the way to the Divine will appear before you.

One Hundred Fourteenth Letter
– Believe

Believe and do good,
Mercy and bounty await,
In faith, find reward.

Embrace the depths of your belief in the Divine. Strengthen your bond with Him. Rely on His guidance and mercy to navigate life's challenges. Pursue virtue. Do acts of kindness and devotion. This will uplift both you and those around you. Seek forgiveness by admitting your mistakes. Seek peace by reconciling with the Divine and others. This will bring harmony and inner peace. Rely on the Divine and trust that He has set provision for you. Trust that the Divine will provide for your needs and guide you through life's trials with wisdom and compassion. Practice gratitude daily. Recognize and appreciate blessings, no matter how small. Live with intention and purpose in your daily activities. Align your actions and aspirations with your values and beliefs. Aim to leave a positive impact on the world. This is guidance for leading a virtuous life. Live a life grounded in belief, forgiveness, and gratitude. This will help foster a deeper connection with the Divine and a more meaningful existence.

One Hundred Fifteenth Letter – Extoll Him

Extol Him at dawn,
and when the night descends low,
praise until sunrise.

No quest for enlightenment can be complete without questing for the Divine. Those who seek purity continually engage in His remembrance. The spiritually enlightened inform us of the significance of remembering the Divine at different times of the day as crucial times for devotion and reflection. They single out certain times because they mark transitions of the different parts of the day. Each transition is a reminder that each moment is an opportunity to contemplate the Divine's blessings and mercy.

Those who seek to complete their purity commence and complete each day with acts of devotion and expressions of gratitude. They cultivate a regular practice of remembrance to acknowledge the Divine's continuous presence throughout our daily experiences.

Take some time to deepen your spiritual connection with the Divine. In doing so, you will develop a profound sense of appreciation and gratitude. This, in turn, will allow you to find solace and direction in your daily life. Integrate reflection on the Divine Entity into your daily routine, and you will find your spiritual journey greatly enhanced.

One Hundred Sixteenth Letter – Bind Him

Bind him in a chain,
Seventy cubits in length,
A fate he must face.

The spiritually deficient do not only face repercussions for their decisions in this life. The overall choice to embrace ignorance and darkness will forever haunt them in the hereafter as well. Their malicious actions stemming from that choice become self-imposed restraints that will ensnare them on the Day of Judgement. These "chains" are the consequences of their own deeds. Their lengths represent the seriousness and gravity of their transgressions. They immobilize themselves in both this world and the hereafter with their own behavior. Their example serves as a cautionary tale. It reminds us that every action we make has consequences. We will be held accountable for the wrong we commit.

It is our responsibility to acknowledge and rectify our actions. We must strive toward moral rectitude in order to lead a truly spiritual life.

One Hundred Seventeenth Letter – Some Listen

Some listen to you,
But can you make the deaf hear?
Understanding lost.

The spiritually enlightened are those who acknowledge their limitations. The Divine's chosen servants could not force the recalcitrant among their people to hear their message. Similarly, we must understand that we cannot compel others to hear or comprehend our viewpoints. Those who seek enlightenment remain focused on their roles by clearly and respectfully communicating their message or opinion. The enlightened recognize that they cannot force anyone to understand or agree. Rather, their responsibility is to beautifully and accurately convey the message. We should refrain from getting frustrated, as people have varying capacities and openness to understanding. Seek guidance and wisdom from the Divine in all of your interactions. Trust that those who are receptive will align themselves with truth and reality.

Practicing patience and empathy is to treat others with kindness and understanding, even if they do not share your perspectives. Patience and empathy will help you communicate effectively, respect other opinions, and rely on divine guidance.

One Hundred Eighteenth Letter
– Obey

Obey your Lord's words,
Follow not other "masters",
Forget not His truth.

The spiritually enlightened rely first and foremost on divine guidance when making decisions in daily life. They are mindful of distractions that can lead one astray, such as societal pressures, personal desires, or harmful habits. By following their example, we can stay focused on our relationship with the Creator and lead more purposeful and fulfilling lives. A dynamic spiritual journey begins once the seekers recognize their weaknesses. Those who seek to complete their purity regularly reflect on their thoughts, words, and actions to ensure that they align with the teachings of the Divine's chosen servants. They remain in the company of supportive people who encourage spiritual growth and guidance in order to strengthen their connection with the Divine. This supportive company is what empowers us to make beneficial decisions, avoid harmful influences, grow in self-awareness and spiritual maturity, and find guidance on our journey. Follow the guidance given by the Divine's chosen servants and the people of enlightenment. Avoid the company of those who brazenly follow their own desires. Prioritize the Divine's guidance, stay focused on the basics of the path, and the deeper realms of spirituality will open up to you.

One Hundred Nineteenth Letter – Hearts Corroded

Hearts so corroded,
lost, By the wages they take,
A soul's heavy cost.

Reflect on your life for a moment. Consider how your past choices and actions may have impacted your relationship with the Divine and your own heart. Spiritually harmful behavior has a corrosive effect. It hardens the heart and distances you from the Divine's guidance. To combat this corrosion, turn your heart to the Divine and seek purity and a fresh start. Cultivate a mindful heart by regularly examining your thoughts, feelings, and actions. Ensure that they align with the Divine's guidance. Prioritize spiritual growth by nurturing the heart and soul through acts of devotion and love for the Divine. Seek the company of positive influences and environments that foster your spiritual well-being. In doing so, you will develop a stronger awareness of your heart's condition. You will cultivate values that prioritize spiritual development. These values will allow you to draw closer to the Divine and His guidance. Seek purification and growth, and you will find fulfillment in life and spirituality.

One Hundred Twentieth Letter – Retaliation

Retaliation,
His aid assured for the just,
Pardoning, Clement.

When you face an affliction or injustice, exercise self-control and restrain yourself from retaliating with similar harm. Instead, defer your grievances to the Divine and trust that He will take care of them, even if you are wronged again. Walk the path of the spiritually enlightened and embrace forgiveness. Choose to pardon and forgive those who have wronged you, as the Divine Himself is pardoning and forgiving. In difficult situations, seek the Divine's help and guidance through acts of devotion and love. Cultivate deeper patience and resilience; they will allow you to endure hardships with the trust that the Divine will see you through. Align yourself with the Divine's attributes of mercy, forgiveness, and justice. Strive to embody these qualities in your own life. By applying these principles, you will develop stronger self-control and patience, along with trust in the Divine. Reflect on the presence of the Divine's attributes in your own life. This leads to a more resilient and spiritually fulfilling life, one that allows you to remain engrossed in awareness of the Divine even in times of hardship.

One Hundred Twenty-First Letter – Seeking

Seeking other "lords",
Divine rules all, futile quest.
Each soul bears its own.

The spiritually enlightened perpetually live in the reality that the Divine is sovereign over all things. They bring others the understanding that each soul is accountable for its own decisions. Therefore, take personal responsibility for your actions and their consequences. Refrain from blaming others for your missteps. Understand that no one else can rectify your errors. Instead, focus on your own spiritual growth and development. Strive to become a better version of yourself. Trust that the Divine will settle all disputes both here and in the hereafter. Seek assistance from divine guidance in navigating life's challenges. By applying this wisdom, you will deepen your understanding of the Divine's sovereignty. Recognizing His authority, taking ownership of your decisions, and trusting in His wisdom will lead to a more spiritually fulfilling life.

One Hundred Twenty-Second Letter – Reading

Reading made simple,
Yet who chooses to study?
Knowledge waits for none.

The spiritually enlightened have given many methods of seeking guidance and wisdom in life. Embrace this wisdom and take advantage of its accessibility and ease of understanding. Strive to learn from the teachings of divine guidance. Reflect regularly on how to apply them in your daily life. Look for opportunities to learn from your experience and truly master the wisdom you possess. Share your knowledge and insights with others to inspire them to do the same. Be open to correction and willing to learn from your mistakes. This will help you cultivate a love for learning and self-improvement. Recognizing the teachings of divine guidance as a lifelong source of wisdom enriches one's life and spirituality. Embracing divine guidance opens the doors to the stations of the path.

One Hundred Twenty-Third Letter – At the Peak

At the peak he soared,
Reaching heights beyond measure,
Limitless ascent.

The enlightened have provided a surefire method for applying divine wisdom in life. It is to reach for the highest standards in all your endeavors. Set lofty goals and work toward achieving them. Never settle for mediocrity in anything you do. Elevate your perspective by looking at life from a higher point of view. Seek wisdom and insight in every experience. Strive for spiritual growth and self-improvement. Use these ideals to nourish your soul and draw closer to the Divine. Work to emulate the spiritually enlightened, those who are embodiments of the Divine's preferred character and beauty. Follow their teachings and gain the tools to empower yourself. Pursue knowledge and the depths of wisdom. Seek understanding and insight. Be a role model for others. Inspire them through your example, just as the previous people of enlightenment inspired others through their love for the Creator. Apply these principles, and you will develop a growth mindset that will prepare you for the deeper stages of the path.

One Hundred Twenty-Fourth Letter – Atoms

Good, like atoms, small,
Yet seen in cosmic balance,
Deeds echo softly.

The enlightened recognize the value of small actions. They view even the smallest of good acts as crucial. They acknowledge the significance of even the most insignificant things. In order to follow their example, you should strive to make consistent kindness a habit. Perform small acts of kindness regularly, knowing that they will accumulate and gain recognition. Be very mindful of your actions. Remember that every one of them, no matter how small, has consequences and accountability. Avail every opportunity to provide benefit to others, as it all has value with the Divine. Encourage others to adopt this mindset. Inspire them to recognize the worth of their actions. Reflect on the positive impact your small actions may have on others. Work to foster the idea that we can contribute to the betterment of all. By applying these principles, you will develop a mindset of kindness and compassion. These are the pillars of enlightenment.

One Hundred Twenty-Fifth Letter – Nature's Reminders

Nature's reminder,
A time of sacred standstill,
His guidance, clear, falls.

The fruit of enlightenment is to treat others with respect and compassion. It is to recognize their temporal and spiritual needs. The key to reaching this point is to prioritize personal hygiene and cleanliness as a sign of respect for oneself and others. Approach relationships with sensitivity and awareness. Recognize the physical and emotional boundaries of others. In navigating relationships and personal matters, turn constantly to the Divine's guidance. Trust in His wisdom and Love. Embrace opportunities for self-reflection and growth. Recognize the value of repentance and self-improvement. Cultivate empathy and understanding toward others, especially during challenging times. Be ready to offer them support when needed. Strive for spiritual growth and closeness to the Divine. Understand that the two are dependent upon recognizing the importance of inner purity and cleanliness. By applying these principles, enlightenment comes within easy reach, and the way to the Creator becomes straight and quick.

One Hundred Twenty-Sixth Letter – Reflect

Reflect on your "gods",
Whom do you truly adore?
Seek truth, worship clear.

The spiritually enlightened guide to the path of removing false idols. Take a moment to reflect on your priorities and values. Consider what you truly worship and prioritize in your life. Ask yourself if your values align with your professed beliefs or if they incline toward worldly desires. Be honest with yourself about any false idols or attachments that may be distracting you from your relationship with the Divine. Once you have identified these areas, reprioritize your focus. Shift your attention to deepening your connection with the Divine and cultivating spiritual growth. Seek guidance from the Divine by seeking His wisdom. Seek the provision He has accorded you and practice gratitude for the blessings in your life. As you do so, strive for contentment and inner peace. Enlightenment lies in the realization that true happiness comes from seeking a stronger connection with the Divine. This connection finds strength in the elimination of false idols.

One Hundred Twenty-Seventh Letter – Neglected Warning

Neglected warning,
Evil shunned, saved from demise,
Justice then prevailed.

As you navigate your life's journey, remember to embrace the Divine's reminders and guidance. Avoid neglecting or ignoring them. Embrace justice and be among those who discourage evil, even when it is challenging. Take time to reflect on your actions and consider their consequences. When you feel yourself veering off of your path, turn back to the Divine with renewed vigor. Learn from your own mistakes as well as the mistakes of others who have neglected the Divine's reminders and persisted in harmful behavior. Seek the Divine's mercy with humility. Continuously strive for spiritual awareness. Avoid spiritually harmful behavior and its consequences. These principles are keys to enlightenment. They unlock the doors to spiritual realities and intimacy with the Divine.

One Hundred Twenty-Eight
Letter – Knowledge

Knowledge awaits you,
Certainty beyond the doubt,
Time will reveal all.

The enlightened teach us that there is immense beauty behind the Divine's timing. The first thing to know is that the Divine's timing is perfect. Therefore, you should step forward and embrace the unknown. Be patient and wait with trust in the Divine; He will reveal the outcome and its wisdoms when the time is right. When the truth becomes clear to you, take the opportunity to reflect on your journey and learn from your experiences. Recognize that the Divine's wisdom and knowledge transcend human understanding. Cultivate inner peace by finding peace in the unknown. Understand that the Divine is in control and will guide you through life's challenges. By applying these principles, you will develop trust and conviction in the Divine. It will help you cultivate spiritually beneficial qualities and embrace the unknown with confidence. Wisdom requires that you undergo a journey of trust in the Divine, and these principles are its stepping stones. This is the start of a beautiful journey that leads to inner peace, enlightenment, and a deep relationship with the Divine Entity.

One Hundred Twenty-Ninth Letter – Creation Unfolds

Creation unfolds,
Night and day in perfect dance,
Guided by His Hand.

The people of enlightenment began their journeys with simple reflections on the nature of creation. As you reflect on the world around you, recognize the Divine's wisdom in creating the universe with reason and purpose. His wisdom transcends human understanding. His creation is but a reflection of His majesty. Take a moment to appreciate the beauty and harmony of nature. See the cycles of the day and night and the movement of the celestial bodies as reminders of the Divine's control and guidance. Just as the day and night are balanced, strive for balance in your own life. Trust in the Divine and be confident in His ability to bestow His mercy and guidance on you. Seek harmony in your relationships and actions. When you err, seek the Divine's forgiveness and mercy. Remember His majesty and guidance. When you apply these principles, you will eventually achieve inner balance and synchronicity with the universe. Balance and harmony with creation serve as the foundation for reflection on the Creator. So, adopt a more mindful and balanced approach to life, and you will find enlightenment awaiting you.

One Hundred Thirtieth Letter – Alone

Alone they will stand,
No aid against Divine Will,
Lost in their own path.

The spiritually enlightened show a path of embracing the Divine's sovereignty. Understand that the Divine Entity is in control of all things. No one can circumvent or change His plans. Trust in His guidance. Be confident that He will show you the right path. Rely on His infinite wisdom and knowledge. Remember that there is no escape from Divine judgment. What matters most is your personal relationship with Him. Seek the Divine's mercy and forgiveness when you fall short. Be mindful of your actions, knowing that they have consequences. Strive to live a spiritually enriching life by avoiding false guidance and misleading influences. Stay true to the Divine's teachings. So, acknowledge the Divine's sovereignty, seek His guidance and mercy, and be mindful of your actions. It will lead you to a more mindful life and greater awareness of the Divine.

One Hundred Thirty-First
Letter – Hands

Hands not reaching out,
Suspicion brews in his mind,
Sent with a message.

The spiritually enlightened have cautioned strongly against the negative opinions of others. When you feel suspicious or fearful of others, take a step back and assess the situation before reacting. Do not jump to conclusions or assume the worst of others without evidence. Instead, communicate openly and honestly. Address your concerns and seek clarity through questions and understanding. Trust in the Divine's wisdom and sovereignty. Understand that everything is under His control. Just as the friends of the Divine show hospitality to their guests, welcome others with kindness and generosity. By applying these principles, you will develop awareness of your thoughts and feelings, avoid making assumptions, and improve your communication skills. You will also have a framework for developing clarity, trust, hospitality, and kindness. Cultivate a mindful approach to relationships, and you will find yourself in harmony with the Divine.

One Hundred Thirty-Second Letter – Disbelief

Disbelief veils sight,
Denial shrouds hardened hearts,
Truth eludes their grasp.

When faced with uncomfortable realities, recognize when you or others are in denial. This denial can pertain to personal issues or truths about the Divine. Be honest with yourself and others. Acknowledge the truth, even if it is difficult. Seek guidance from the Divine's wisdom and turn to others for help when you need it. Avoid being stubborn and resistant to change and new ideas. Instead, welcome the truth with an open heart and mind. Be willing to learn and grow. Share the truth with others, but do so with compassion and respect. By applying these principles, you will develop a strong sense of honesty with yourself. This is a rare and beautiful strength that helps you embrace the truth even when it is challenging. It is the tool that allows you to fully imbibe the teachings of the path that leads one to enlightenment and the Divine Presence.

One Hundred Thirty-Third Letter – Great Bounty

Great bounty descends,
Regret whispers in the heart,
Filled with lost chances.

When you notice yourself taking the Divine's blessings and favors for granted, do your best to recognize the ingratitude. Make a conscious effort to change. Remember that everything good finds its origin in the Divine. Acknowledge His role in your life. Remain humble and grateful for what you have. Refrain from attributing success solely to your own efforts. Do not waste your time fantasizing what could have been if you were in someone else's shoes. Instead, focus on your own journey and progress. Comparison and fantasizing will eventually lead to discontentment. Keep your eyes fixed on your path and use the Divine's blessings to benefit others. By applying these principles, you will develop a grateful heart. This quality allows you to recognize the Divine's sovereignty. It will also keep you humble and grounded and help you show generosity to others. These strengths are all key ingredients for awareness of the ultimate reality. The openness of a grateful heart always makes space for the Divine Presence.

One Hundred Thirty-Fourth Letter – Prayers Rise

Prayers rise, hands stretched,
Blessings shared, provisions spent,
Acts of faith commend.

Prayer is both a form and a reality. The spiritually enlightened have disclosed the method of using one to reach the other. Start by establishing a strong habit of reflection by prioritizing your spiritual growth through regular rituals of devotion. Be mindful of the blessings and provisions the Divine has given you. Express gratitude for what you have. Share your resources with others. This can be through charity, volunteering, or simply supporting those who need it. Cultivate a generous and sharing spirit. Strike a balance between your private rituals and worldly responsibilities. At the same time, trust wholeheartedly in the Divine's abundance. These procedures will deepen your spiritual connection. They will help you acknowledge and appreciate the Divine's blessings. They will also help develop an openhearted mindset, which will help you cultivate contentment in the heart and soul. Prayer, when done in this manner, helps you lead a fulfilling life. It also sets the stage for higher levels of spiritual awareness.

One Hundred Thirty-Fifth
Letter – Blame

Blame rests on those who
Seek exemption though wealthy,
Content to stay back.

Those who seek to complete their purity are never content with putting their spiritual development on the back burner. Take a moment to reflect on your actions and motivations. Ask yourself if you are truly committed to your ideals and values. Consider whether you are prioritizing comfort and ease over spiritual growth and service to others. Take time to be honest with yourself. Are you seeking exemptions and excuses to avoid responsibilities, or are you embracing challenges and opportunities for growth?

Be aware of hypocritical tendencies within yourself. Recognize whether you seek special treatment while claiming to be a follower of divine guidance. Hold yourself accountable for actions and words. Encourage authenticity and integrity in others. Remember, spiritual growth and responsibility are the keys to developing deep and meaningful convictions.

Embrace challenges and opportunities for spiritual growth. Take responsibility for your own spiritual journey and development. Do not rely on others to carry the burden for you. Instead, seek knowledge, wisdom, and spiritual growth with an open heart and mind. Show compassion and empathy toward those who are struggling or truly in need. Encourage them as well to take responsibility for their own spiritual growth.

Seek the company of a supportive community that encourages spiritual growth and accountability. Work to become a source of support and guidance for others. Help create an environment where seekers can grow and learn together. Remember that, most importantly, the Divine's mercy and guidance are available to all. Work to embrace these principles as their fruits will lead you to further heights and ever closer to the ultimate goal.

One Hundred-Thirty Sixth
Letter – No Fault

No fault enters in
Unoccupied homes you find,
He knows all concealed.

Those who seek purity begin their path by becoming cognizant of the rights of others. They learn the importance of respecting other people's property and privacy. We should be mindful of entering someone's home or space without permission, even if it is unoccupied. Always seek permission or clarification before entering a space that does not belong to you. Furthermore, we should work to cultivate integrity and honesty in our dealings with others. Avoid hiding or concealing the truth. We should strive to be truthful and sincere in our words and actions. We must recognize that the Divine knows our actions, intentions, and innermost secrets.

The path to purity continues in the recognition that we are accountable for our lives, choices, and consequences. We should be mindful of how our actions impact others and the world around us. We must trust in the Divine to show us the right path. By seeking guidance from the Divine through prayer and reflection, we can cultivate deeper conviction in His Knowledge and guidance. When we cultivate these qualities within ourselves, we eventually find the path to complete our purity. It is this purity that leads to enlightenment and the Divine Presence.

One Hundred Thirty-Seventh Letter – True

True to Him alone,
Associates drift away,
Lost in distant winds.

There is no enlightenment without belief in the Absolute One, the Creator of the Universe, the Divine Entity. Those who walk the path begin with this immutable tenet. Focus on strengthening your belief in the oneness of the Divine. Recognize His unity and uniqueness in all aspects of your life. Avoid associating any partners or rivals with Him. Refrain from attributing His Power or attributes to anyone or anything else. Regularly examine your intentions and motivations. Ensure that they align with the Divine's pleasure. Seek to please Him in all of your actions. Trust that the Divine, in His limitless power, will protect and guide you, even in uncertain or challenging situations. Cultivate humility and gratitude. Acknowledge the Divine's blessings and favors in your life. Stay grounded and aware of your limitations. Rely on His strength and guidance. By focusing on the oneness of the Divine in this manner, you can immensely deepen your connection with Him. Maintain a pure and sincere relationship with the Divine, free from any form of polytheism, and the path to enlightenment will open its highest doors to you.

One Hundred Thirty-Eighth Letter – Believers Beware

Believers, beware,
Friends of Divine, not despair,
Hope beyond the grave.

The enlightened tell us that the great majority of one's spirituality amounts to the company one keeps. It is crucial to be mindful of your company and the influences in your life. Avoid befriending or closely associating with individuals who have rejected the Divine's guidance and have no firm belief in the hereafter. Their negative influences can hinder your spiritual growth. Instead, seek the company of those who share your values and support your spiritual growth. Seek guidance from knowledgeable and wise people who can help you deepen your connection with the Divine. Additionally, limit your exposure to harmful or corrupting influences that may lead you astray. Protect your spirituality and values by avoiding environments that may tempt you to compromise your beliefs.

Keep your focus on the hereafter and the everlasting consequences of your actions. Prioritize your spiritual growth and development. Seek to please the Divine in all aspects of your life. Use your connection with the Divine to become a wellspring of compassion and kindness. Even though you should avoid negative influences, do not shy away from sharing knowledge and wisdom with others. Always remember to be gentle and understanding when providing guidance to others. These principles of good company will allow you to deepen your conviction and support others on their spiritual journeys. The fruit of prioritizing your own journey will be to provide benefit to others.

One Hundred Thirty-Ninth
Letter – Man

Man, witness to self,
Deeds unveiled and truth revealed,
Echoes of his soul.

The spiritually enlightened have shown us through their words and actions that the journey to the Divine begins with the journey to one's own heart. Start by practicing self-reflection. Examine your thoughts, words, and actions regularly. Be honest with yourself. Realize your strengths and accept your weaknesses. Strive to improve upon your positive qualities. Take ownership of your decisions and choices. Recognize that you are responsible for your own life. Avoid blaming others or making excuses. Instead, use your mistakes as growing and learning experiences.

Listen to the voice of your heart. Allow it to guide you to its natural disposition of spiritual and moral integrity. Cultivate this integrity further by seeking guidance from the Divine and His wisdom in your daily life. Remember that you will stand before the Divine on the Day of Judgement. Therefore, you should strive to live a life pleasing to the Divine. Seek His mercy and forgiveness when you falter. When you find yourself applying these principles deeply, you will know that your journey has begun.

One Hundred Fortieth Letter – True Virtue

True virtue achieved,
In giving what is held dear,
He sees every act.

No one can travel the path without having an openhearted attitude. Those who seek any station on the path must learn to integrate it into their basic nature. Start by practicing generosity and charity. Share your resources with others, especially those in need. Trust that the Divine is aware of your actions. Generosity can include sharing your wealth, time, or skills. Its essence is to recognize that true virtue lies in letting go of what you hold dear and trusting in the Divine. This is a sacred tool for strengthening your conviction in the Almighty in both this life and the next. Additionally, show compassion and empathy toward others. Work to understand their struggles and challenges. Give from what you cherish. The more you value it, the more joy and relief it can bring to those in need. Finally, practice gratitude for what you have. Give what you have with humility. Enlightenment stems from the realization that everything you have is a blessing from the Divine. The best way to show gratitude for these blessings is to pay them forward.

One Hundred Forty-First Letter – Their Presence

Their presence, unclear,
Do they bring benefit, harm?
Questions, lingering.

Take a moment to think about the people in your life. Your relationships with them can have a huge impact on your well-being and spiritual growth. Are they people who uplift and support others? Do they bring others down and mislead them? One must consider these questions seriously with an open mind and an honest heart.

This same reflection applies to the influences in your life—the media you consume, the groups you belong to, and the ideas you expose yourself to. Do they nourish your soul and those of others, and do they inspire you to be your best selves? Do they leave you feeling empty, anxious, or lost?

You have the power to choose who and what you let into your life. You can set boundaries with those who harm or hinder your growth. You can seek out those who support and benefit your journey. Do not cut out everyone who challenges you. Rather, prioritize the company of those who truly benefit your spiritual growth. These choices are not always easy, but they are essential for your spiritual, mental, and even physical well-being.

Seek support from those who uplift you. Seek guidance from mentors, role models, or spiritual leaders who have walked the path before you. Cultivate relationships and influences that nourish your soul and inspire you to grow.

By being mindful and intentional about whom and what you allow into your life, you can create a supportive environment that nurtures spiritual growth and overall well-being for everyone.

One Hundred Forty-Second
Letter – Stars

Stars twinkle, trees bow,
In silent reverence, they
Prostrate to the One.

The majesty of the Divine and the beauty of His creation are not easily lost on the mind. Imagine standing under a vast starlit sky, feeling the Earth beneath your feet. Or, picture yourself in a quiet forest surrounded by towering trees. These are real scenes present in the world that truly evoke wonder in the heart. Reflect on your experiences with the natural world in order to cultivate a sense of humility and gratitude for the beauty and blessings in your life. Spend more time observing the natural world. Contemplate the beauty and majesty of what you see of the stars, trees, and oceans. Recognize the interconnectedness of all creation and your place within it. View the prostration of the stars and trees as a reminder of the importance of spiritual growth and devotion. Strive to emulate their humility and submission to the Divine. Practice both mindfulness and wonder in your daily life. Appreciate the majesty and beauty of the Divine's creation. Allow this sense of wonder to inspire you to grow closer to the Divine. It is a precious quality that will allow you to live a mindful and grateful life. Wonder felt from what the eyes behold inevitably opens the doors of the heart.

One Hundred Forty-Third
Letter – Repentance

Repentance sincere,
Received by the Merciful,
Hearts find peace anew.

No one can walk the path without feeling the weight of their regrets. Many of you probably feel heavyhearted and burdened by the weight of your mistakes and missteps. I am here to tell you that there is hope. There is certainly a way to spiritual levity and peace. It starts with forgiveness. It is forgiveness from the Divine, that Entity who loves you unconditionally. It is also forgiveness from those you have wronged.

Seek forgiveness with sincerity. Pour your heart out to the Divine and those whom you have hurt. Resolve to leave behind the harmful habits and behaviors that have led you down a dark path. Take concrete steps to make amends and repair the damage you have caused. It will not be easy, but I promise you, it is worth the effort.

Declare your devotion and commitment to the Divine openly. Share your story of transformation with others. Embrace the Divine's infinite mercy and compassion. Trust in His promise to accept your repentance and celebrate your return to Him. Start anew, leaving your past mistakes behind, used only as reminders to avoid. Strive to live a life that pleases the Divine, filled with gratitude and humility.

This is the process to experience the pure joy of forgiveness, the deep peace of making amends, and the comforting embrace of the Divine's mercy. You will feel a lightness, a sense of freedom you might have thought impossible. Remember that the Divine is intently waiting to receive your repentance and guide you on your journey back to Him.

It is never too late to turn toward the Divine and start fresh. So, take that first step, open your heart to the idea of forgiveness, and prepare to walk the path of transformation and growth. You will inevitably come to realize that you are loved, you are redeemable, and that the Divine is with you every step of the way.

One Hundred Forty-Fourth Letter – Open Skies

Beneath open skies,
Provision awaits the just,
Destiny's embrace.

Imagine this: you are standing at the edge of a vast, unknown territory, a territory called "Trust in the Divine's orovision." You are unsure of what lies ahead, and the uncertainty is rather unsettling. However, deep within, you feel a nudge, a whisper, saying, "This is the way forward. Trust. I will provide."

My friends, that is the journey we are all on. It is the journey of learning to trust in the Divine's provision, to have faith that He will supply all of our needs. Let me tell you, it is a journey that is full of challenges and blessings in equal measure. I have traveled this journey for a while now, and I have learned a few things along the way. First of all, trust is a choice. It is a decision you make every day, every moment. You choose to believe that the Divine will provide, even if things are unclear to you, like a path shrouded in fog. You choose to firmly believe, even when doubt creeps in.

You know what? That choice matters. When you choose to trust, you open the door for the Divine to work in your life in ways you cannot even imagine. When you choose firm belief over doubt, you tap into a source of strength and peace that defies human understanding. However, trust is not just about sitting back and waiting for miracles. It is about taking action, doing your part, and leaving the results of your efforts to the Divine. It is about working hard, striving for your goals, and then surrendering the outcome. It is about being patient and recognizing that the Divine's timing is perfect, even when it feels delayed. You know what else? Trust is about gratitude. It is about recognizing the blessings that are already in your life. It is about realizing the ways that the Divine has already provided. When you cultivate a heart full of gratitude, you will find that even in the leanest times, there is always something to be grateful for.

Finally, trust is about sharing. It is about realizing that the Divine has blessed you so that you can be a blessing to others. It is about giving generously, even when it feels like you do not have much to give. When you give from a place of trust, you tap into an abundance that defies logic. My friends, trusting in the Divine's provision is a journey, not a destination. There will be days when it comes easily and days when it feels impossible. However, through it all, the Divine is with you. He sees you. He loves you. So, choose trust. Choose belief. Work hard, be patient, give thanks, and share generously. In the process, you will discover a peace that transcends understanding and a joy that withstands all circumstances.

The Divine is good. He is faithful. He is the ultimate Provider. Trust in Him, and you will never be disappointed.

One Hundred Forty-Fifth Letter – Forgiven

Forgiven, he finds
Nearness to divine embrace,
A homecoming grace.

The path to a deeper relationship with the Divine begins with sincerely seeking His forgiveness. Forgiveness is not just something to remedy mistakes but also lapses in our remembrance of the Divine. Recognize these mistakes and lapses. Ask for His mercy and pardon, just as His friends did before you. This repentance opens the door to His boundless grace. Once you have done that, strive to draw nearer to the Divine through devotion, worship, and beneficial acts. Prioritize your relationship with Him about all else, and you will begin to feel a profound sense of connection and peace. Live with the hope and expectation of a good outcome in the hereafter. Believe that your efforts to please the Divine will be rewarded with honor and appreciation. Draw inspiration from the stories of the spiritually enlightened and their experiences with forgiveness and nearness to the Divine. Strive to follow their example. This process is the method to experience the hidden joys of the spiritual path. Remember that the Divine is always willing to forgive and bring you close. He promises a good outcome for those who strive to please Him. Striving in this way opens the doors to a deeper spirituality that transcends the self and finds its roots in the joys found beyond this realm.

One Hundred Forty-Sixth Letter – Dark Whispers

From dark whispers, Lord,
Grant me refuge, keep me safe,
In Your light, I rest.

No traveler on the path is free from temptation. When faced with such temptation or negative thoughts, it is important to stay mindful and aware of your emotions and thought patterns. Recognize when unhelpful or harmful thoughts arise. Make a conscious effort to reject them. Replace them with positive and uplifting perspectives. Seek the company of supportive people who can provide wise counsel and encouragement. Seek out resources that inspire and motivate you to stay true to your values and principles. Cultivate practices that help you maintain inner peace and clarity. Remember that you have the power to think through your thoughts and choose your actions. By being vigilant and resilient, you can overcome negativity and stay on a path of personal growth. Seek guidance from those whom you trust and respect. Trust in your own ability to make positive choices that align with your highest ideals.

One Hundred Forty-Seventh Letter – Mysteries

Mysteries unfold,
In letters, secrets untold,
Alif, Laam, Meem, bold.

"Alif, Lam, Meem" invites us to reflect on the mysteries of the Divine, symbolized by these enigmatic letters. As we ponder the wonders of the world around us, we find reminders of the secrets that lie beyond human understanding. These mysteries serve as another reminder to seek guidance and wisdom from the Divine. The enlightened trust Him to always deliver favorable outcomes. In times of uncertainty or difficulty, we can find comfort and solace in the Word of the Divine. By embracing this reality, we can deepen our appreciation for creation and connect more deeply to divine wisdom. Ultimately, "Alif, Lam, Meem" serves as a powerful reminder of the mystery that surrounds the Divine Entity. It is a mystery that those traveling the path of His love spend their lives unraveling.

One Hundred Forty-Eighth
Letter – Revival

Oath of Revival,
Day of Judgment proclaimed firm,
Truth's solemn promise.

The enlightened will never fail to remind us that we will be held accountable for our actions. Reflecting on the Day of Resurrection can inspire us to make better choices and live a more spiritually healthy life. Realizing that our actions have consequences that will be weighed on that day, we should prioritize performing beneficial actions and avoiding harmful ones. Remembering our inevitable accountability for our thoughts, words, and actions can help us stay mindful and firm on our path. Moreover, seeking forgiveness and mercy from the Divine for our mistakes can bring us peace and solace. Understanding the significance of the Day of Resurrection can also inspire us to take responsibility for our lives. We can thus make amends for past mistakes and work toward a better future. Ultimately, we must remember that the Day of Resurrection marks the start of everlasting life. Therefore, we should prioritize our spiritual growth and the pursuit of everlasting happiness. By applying these principles, the mysterious nature of the world that lies beyond will begin to dissipate. What started as conjecture in the mind will cement into belief in the heart. This belief and conviction are the foundations of spiritual travel.

One Hundred Forty-Ninth Letter – Submission

Submission's pure call,
Some stand firm, while others wane,
In rectitude found.

There are many among humanity who have placed their feet on the path. Among them, very few have actually started their journey. Among them, very few have continued. Among them, a very small number have reached enlightenment. Among them, even fewer have made it to the Divine Presence. This journey is one that requires high aspiration and determination. The key to unlocking these virtues is submission. Embracing a state of submission to the Divine's Will and guidance is itself a lifelong journey. As you strive to submit, aim to live a life in line with the spiritual path. Make choices that align with divine commands and values. Avoid compromising your beliefs and values. Instead, stand firm in your principles. Regularly reflect on your intentions. Ensure that they align with your commitment to submission and virtue. When faced with challenges or uncertainty, seek guidance from the Divine. Seek the company of like-minded individuals who share your commitment to submission and virtue and who support and encourage each other on this path. Embrace the reality of accountability. Realize that your actions have consequences and that you will be held accountable for your choices. Strive for consistency in your submission and virtue, even in the face of difficulty or temptation. By embracing this path, you will deepen your level of commitment to the Creator and the path that leads to Him. When you embrace the principles of submission, you unlock the secrets of determination.

One Hundred Fiftieth Letter – Crescents

Crescents guide us well,
Timetables and Pilgrim's call,
Peace in piety.

The spiritually enlightened underscore the importance of entering people's homes through their front doors. This means respecting people's privacy and physical boundaries and always seeking permission before entering another's home. The enlightened also emphasize the importance of approaching life situations and relationships with honesty, integrity, and respect. This means being honest and transparent in your dealings with others. It means respecting people's emotional boundaries and privacy. It means approaching challenges and opportunities with a positive and virtuous mindset. It also means prioritizing spiritual growth in your actions and decisions and seeking to build strong, respectful relationships with others. Remember, Divine wisdom is timeless and universal. Its applications can be adapted to various aspects of life. It will guide us to a more virtuous and beneficial path.

One Hundred Fifty-First Letter – Creator

He's the Creator,
With Him all power resides,
Sufficient for me.

As you reflect on your beliefs and actions, ask yourself if you are attributing power or control to anyone or anything besides the Divine. Remember that the Divine is the ultimate Creator and Sustainer of the universe. Affirm your faith in His sovereignty and mercy. Recognize that only the Divine has the power to harm or benefit you. Trust that His plans are always to your benefit, even if you do not understand them. Cultivate a sense of reliance on the Divine. Strengthen the belief that He is sufficient for you.

Relinquish attachments to people, material possessions, and status. Remember that these things are not lasting sources of comfort or security. Practice detachment and trust in the Divine's provision and guidance. As you do so, you will develop a sense of inner strength and resilience. You will be able to face challenges with courage and the belief that the Divine is with you. Find comfort in the knowledge that the Divine's mercy and blessings are always available to you.

Share the wisdom you gain with others in a respectful and compassionate way. Encourage them to reflect on their own beliefs and dependencies. Be a source of comfort and support for those who are struggling. This path invites you to deepen your faith, trust, and reliance on the Divine and to share that with others. Traveling the path will take you toward a more profound connection with your Creator and a more fulfilling life.

One Hundred Fifty-Second
Letter – Gathering Them All

Gathering them all,
They will all surely soon see,
Justice of their deeds.

A major component of enlightenment is the realization of harm. As you reflect on your relationships and interactions with others, consider whether you have exploited or harmed anyone. You should also consider whether others have exploited or harmed you, and forgive them. Take responsibility for your actions and acknowledge the harm caused. Recognize that your actions have consequences and impact others. We are accountable not only for our own actions but also for the actions of those we support or follow. So, be mindful of the company you keep and the influences in your life.

Our actions have consequences that pertain to this life as well as the hereafter. Fire is an allusion to suffering and disgrace. It is used as a consequence of our choices. However, the Divine's mercy and forgiveness are always available. Strive to make amends and seek forgiveness when you have wronged others. Trust in the Divine's wisdom. Understand that He is Aware of all circumstances. Trust that the Divine's plan is to guide humanity toward virtue and compassion. Seek guidance and wisdom from the Divine in your daily life.

Use this principle as a reminder to continually reflect and improve yourself. Strive to be a positive influence on those around you. Do your best to support justice and compassion. Seek to break free from harmful cycles and patterns. Work toward personal growth and reform. Implement this principle, and you will be guided to the deepest wisdoms of the path.

One Hundred Fifty-Third Letter – Your Shelter

In Your shelter, Lord,
I find solace from darkness,
Shield me from evil.

Feeling overwhelmed by life's challenges? We all face temptations and doubts that can lead us away from our path. However, there is a powerful tool you can use to stay centered, focused, and connected to the Divine. It is simply to say, "I seek refuge with the Divine from the accursed Satan."

These simple yet powerful words can be your shield against harmful influences. Say it when you wake up in the morning to set a positive intention for your day. Say it when you go to bed at night to dispel any negativity you may have encountered.

When you face temptations or difficult choices, pause and seek refuge in the Divine by saying these words. This statement will help you resist the urgings of evil influences. It will aid you in staying true to your values. Include it in your daily activities to deepen your connection with the Divine.

One Hundred Fifty-Fourth Letter – They Lived

They lived for the now,
Not future, blind to the seeds
sowing in the sand.

Feeling like your life is out of control? It is easy to get caught up in the hustle and bustle of daily life, like a ship lost at sea. However, there is a way to regain a sense of direction and purpose: living with accountability.

Accountability means recognizing that your actions have consequences and taking ownership of them. It is about being mindful of your choices and considering how they may impact yourself and others. By living with accountability, you can prepare for the future by making intentional decisions that align with your values and aspirations.

How does one incorporate a sense of accountability? Start by regularly reflecting on your actions and their outcomes. When you make mistakes, as we all do, take responsibility for them without blaming others or the circumstances. Make amends where necessary. Use these experiences as opportunities for learning and growth.

Stay humble. Acknowledge that you are not perfect. Remain open to guidance from wise counsel, mentors, and self-reflection. Ask yourself, "Are my actions leading me closer to my goals, or further away?"

This principle allows you to strengthen your connection with your authentic self. What's more, it allows you to forge an authentic connection of love with your Creator. Remember, your actions today shape tomorrow, so live with intention and purpose.

One Hundred Fifty-Fifth Letter – Mysterious Ways

Mysterious ways,
He beyond questioning stands,
Human hearts answer.

Feeling overwhelmed by life's uncertainties? It is natural to question and doubt when things do not go as planned. However, there is a source of comfort and guidance that is easily available to you. It is trust in the Divine's wisdom. We must realize that His wisdom is beyond human understanding. Let go of doubts and questions about the Divine's actions or decisions. Focus instead on your own actions and responsibilities. Embrace the fact that you will be held accountable for your choices. Make conscious decisions accordingly. Regularly reflect on your actions and motives. Make amends where necessary.

Seek guidance from the Divine's wisdom through His Word. Seek it from knowledgeable and virtuous individuals as well. Focus on humility by recognizing your limitations and acknowledging that you do not have all the answers. Prioritize building your own virtue and a strong relationship with the Divine. When these principles take root in the heart, all of your innate positive qualities begin to shine from within. Ultimately, remember that your actions and choices are what matter, and you will face their consequences, good or ill.

One Hundred Fifty-Sixth Letter – Empty Bellies

Empty bellies ache,
Hope's sustenance on the brink,
Feeding souls in need.

Feeling moved to make a difference in the world but not sure where to start? There is a simple answer. Begin by sharing what you have, even if it is just a little bit. Sharing your resources, showing compassion, and volunteering your time can make a significant difference in the lives of those struggles.

Be willing to share your food, wealth, and resources with those in need, especially during times of crisis or hardship. This does not simply mean that you should donate money to large causes. You can also help out locally in your own community. You can start with your own home and relatives. Demonstrate kindness and empathy toward those who are struggling. Offer support in any way you can.

Involve yourself in local organizations that help feed the hungry and provide for those in need. Share your blessings with others, even if it is just a small act of kindness. This can be something like buying someone a meal or offering a snack to a friend in need. It can even be listening to someone with an open heart. Practice self-reflection by recognizing your own blessings. Acknowledge the times when you have experienced hunger or struggle. Use those experiences to empathize with others.

Furthermore, support efforts to address hunger and poverty both locally and globally. These principles of social responsibility are, in reality, opportunities to search for and connect with the Divine. They will serve as an excellent foundation for an authentic relationship with the Creator.

One Hundred Fifty-Seventh Letter – Illness

Hearts veiled in illness,
Fear and suspicion entwine,
Unjust within them.

Take a moment to pause and turn inward. Reflect on your deepest intentions and examine your heart. Are there doubts, suspicions, or fears lurking within that are driving your actions? Let go of the negative thoughts that cloud your belief. Cast aside the assumptions that cause you to question the Divine's infinite Justice and the wisdom of His friends. Instead, trust the Divine to carry you forward to your best interests. Seek guidance from the timeless wisdom of His words and the teachings of those who bring you closer to Him. Recognize your own flaws and weaknesses with compassion. Understand that we are all works of art in progress. Strive to improve yourself. Do so by treating others with the justice, respect, and kindness that they deserve. These principles are the ailments to the illnesses of the heart. Applying them will allow you to overcome the shadows of doubt and become a beacon of light in the world. The Divine is always just and fair. By surrendering to His guidance, you can find the peace, clarity, and purpose that your soul craves.

One Hundred Fifty-Eight Letter – His People

His people refused,
Messengers' words dismissed cold,
Belief they forswore.

Those who walk the path learn the value of experience gained from error. They gain valuable insight from their own missteps as well as the missteps of others. To learn from the mistakes of others, begin by opening your heart to guidance and wisdom from all corners of life. When you encounter new ideas or perspectives, resist the urge to reject them outright simply because they challenge your existing beliefs or lifestyle. Instead, listen with an open mind and receptive heart. Realize that there is always room for growth and evolution. Study the stories of individuals and communities who have navigated similar challenges. Reflect on their mistakes and triumphs. Embrace humility. Acknowledge your own limitations and biases. Seek knowledge and understanding from diverse sources. This will equip you to make informed decisions and navigate life's complexities with grace and wisdom. Remember that your actions ripple out into the world. So, strive to live a life that uplifts others and nurtures the well-being of the community. Developing a receptive heart is the bedrock for learning and commitment to personal growth and development. This is the path to wisdom, compassion, and a life of purpose and meaning.

One Hundred Fifty-Ninth Letter – Success

Success in cleansing,
Purity found in the soul,
True triumph resides.

To apply the principle of self-purification, begin by taking time to reflect on your thoughts, words, and actions. Examine your inner self. Identify areas where you can improve. Work to purify your mind and heart. Let go of harmful habits and behaviors that hold you back; make a conscious effort to overcome them. Strive to cultivate good character by developing virtues like compassion, honesty, and kindness. Before acting, take a moment to purify your intentions. Ensure that they align with your values and principles. Seek self-improvement through activities that promote personal growth, such as learning new skills or seeking knowledge. Be responsible for your physical, mental, and emotional well-being by developing healthy habits and seeking help when needed. When you make mistakes, acknowledge them, seek forgiveness, and use them as opportunities for growth. These principles are the framework for purifying the body, heart, and soul. Embrace the process and acknowledge your capacity to grow. Your heart is capable of immense transformation. With each passing day, you can draw closer to your highest potential. The path of purification is not always easy, but it is always worthwhile. Have the courage to face your flaws, the humility to seek improvement, and the love to keep growing. This is the path to inner peace, outer harmony, and recognition of the Creator.

One Hundred Sixtieth Letter – Guidance Lost

Guidance lost to Him,
Blundering in transgression,
Stray without a guide.

Seeking the Divine's guidance is a journey of faith, submission, and connection. It is not a passive wait for answers but an active process of opening ourselves to His wisdom. This means starting each day by acknowledging His Almighty Presence. It is to ask for direction and strength for whatever comes your way. It means being mindful of your actions, striving to live in alignment with your values, and having the courage to course-correct when you stray. Seeking guidance requires humility, vulnerability, and a willingness to be led. In this submission, you will find incredible freedom and a profound sense of purpose. You will develop a sense that your life is like a fabric that is part of a larger cloth, woven with care and intention. Even in the darkest threads, you will know in your heart that the Divine is present, guiding you, shaping you, and leading you to a light that you cannot yet see. This is a journey of constant course correction. With each step taken, you will find a little more peace and a little more clarity. In those moments, you will know that it's exactly where you are meant to be, safe in His protection.

One Hundred Sixty-First Letter – Resurrection

Resurrection's dawn,
Deeds unveiled, remembered clear,
Lord, the Witness True.

Imagine you are about to make a decision, and no one else is around to see what you choose. Maybe it is a small thing, like whether to tell the truth or a little white lie. Maybe it is something bigger, like whether to help someone in need or turn away. In those moments, it can be tempting to think that what we do does not matter because no one will know. However, the Divine knows, and in the end, that is what matters most.

This path is one of friendship with the Divine. You can cower in fear and apprehension of impending judgment, or you can embrace this reality and look beyond shortsighted emotions. When we travel the path of friendship, we come to understand the wisdoms and kindnesses behind the realities that form the basics of the path. Our superficial devotion to the Creator becomes loyalty to a friend who wants only the best for us. Turn this Divine witness into your best friend. Find the best possible solution to this chronic loneliness that ails your heart. Beyond the veils of your thoughts, emotions, and the wonders of existence, He awaits you.

One Hundred Sixty-Second
Letter – Prayer

Prayer for pardon,
Parents and believers joined,
Reckoning's embrace.

The kind of world we want to create is one where we consciously seek forgiveness and extend mercy to others. We are all flawed, all struggling in our own ways. Despite this, we can find peace and connection when we approach others with kindness and understanding. When we remember to seek forgiveness and have compassion for those around us, we open ourselves up to a deeper sense of connection and purpose.

The friends of the Divine understood this reality. They extended love to relatives and even strangers. They recognize that we are all the best of the Divine's creation, deserving of His Mercy. We can follow their example by extending special love to our families, our friends, and even those who challenge us. When we ask the Divine to forgive and guide others, we cultivate a heart of compassion and humility. This compassion is the key to a meaningful life. It allows us to see beyond our own concerns and recognize the shared humanity of those around us. When we treat others with kindness, we create a ripple effect that can touch countless lives. When we inevitably make mistakes, we can find solace in the knowledge that the Divine's forgiveness is always available to us.

So, as you navigate your daily life, remember to seek forgiveness and extend mercy. Extend love and attention to those around you, even those who may seem different or difficult. Approach others with kindness and humility, recognizing that we are all on this journey together. By doing so, you will contribute to a world where compassion and understanding can heal divisions and bring us closer to the love and grace of the Divine.

One Hundred Sixty-Third
Letter – Eyes

Eyes open to signs,
Pharaoh's doom foreseen ahead,
Heavens' Lord decrees.

You know how sometimes in life, it feels like you are wandering without a map? In such moments, you should recognize that it is time to remember the signs. Just like how you might spot a trail marker in the wilderness, the Divine's signs are always around us to remind us of His presence and guidance. When you feel lost or overwhelmed, take a moment to pause and look for those signs. Turn to the Divine for direction and wisdom, just like you would consult a compass. Trust in His infinite knowledge and mercy, even when the path is unclear.

Let me tell you a tale from my earlier days on this path. I was faced with a huge decision and felt paralyzed by uncertainty. I sought guidance from the Divine. In the moments that followed, a sense of peace washed over me. It was as if the Divine was saying, "Trust me, even when you cannot see the way forward." That moment of submission gave me the courage to move forward. Sure enough, the path unfolded from there, one step at a time.

We all have the choice to either follow the way of the Divine's friends, or the way of those who stood against Him. When confronted with challenges, do we stand up for truth and justice, even in times of difficulty, or do we let fear and pride mislead us? Humility, trust, and courage are the qualities that will light the way.

More often than not, we will have the sense that we know how to manage our own affairs the best. However, the path of enlightenment teaches us that the Divine's management of affairs is so much greater than what we can comprehend. The spark that ignites our souls lights up when we let go of arrogance and obstinacy in exchange for a willingness to learn and grow. That is when we become instruments of the Divine's love and light in the world.

One Hundred Sixty-Fourth Letter – A Thousand Angels

A thousand angels,
Sent to reinforce the call,
Divine aid descends.

The spiritually enlightened constantly receive and give reminders of the Divine's presence in our lives. When you face challenges or difficulties, remember that you are never alone. The Divine is always with you, ready to provide the support and guidance you need. Trust in His love and wisdom. Believe that He is with you every step of the way.

You may not see it, but the Divine's servants are present with you as well. They are vessels of His protection and assistance.

Find strength in the support of fellow people on the path and community members. Lean on each other, just as the friends of the Divine did. Give thanks for the Divine's blessings in your life, especially in the midst of hardship.

Keep a positive attitude. Realize that the Divine works for your best interests. Draw strength from His support and continue your journey, even when the going gets tough. He has guided His chosen servants and friends through extreme trials; He will certainly guide you too.

Apply these wisdoms to cultivate positivity within yourself. Positivity is the bedrock of determination. Determination is what one needs to reach the true goal of the path.

One Hundred Sixty-Fifth Letter – Commands

Commands followed through,
Distributing as decreed,
Obedience shown.

The Divine has never left any of us bereft of examples in our own lives that evoke His remembrance. They do not have to be major or extreme; in fact, that is seldom the case. It could be as simple as the generosity of our elders. Perhaps they were people who, no matter how little they had, were always giving something to those in need. Perhaps they taught you that generosity is not restricted to material wealth; it also applies to sharing your time and talents. I have found such examples in my own life, and they have left a deep impression on me. As I have grown older, I have come to understand that this kind of selflessness is at the heart of our path.

As spiritual travelers, we have a duty to be generous and compassionate. We are called to share our resources with others. This is not simply to fulfill an obligation; it is to cultivate a mindset of love and service to creation. When we give freely and selflessly, we are not just alleviating immediate suffering. We are also sowing the seeds of a more equitable and just society.

There are many ways to practice generosity in our daily lives. Giving to the poor and needy is essential, but we can also share our skills and time with those who could benefit from them. Every act of kindness counts.

The more we give, the more we open ourselves up to the Divine's blessings and guidance.

Generosity is not limited to acts of kindness. It can also be about making sacrifices and stepping outside of our comfort zones. However, you will surely find that the more you give, the more fulfilling your life will become. When you focus on serving others, the Divine has a way of multiplying your blessings in ways you cannot imagine.

The point is not to try and fix everything on our own. The point is to do our part and to be a source of benefit for others. When we act from a place of love, the Divine has a way of amplifying our efforts. When we give selflessly, we become instruments of His mercy and compassion.

One Hundred Sixty-Sixth Letter
– Believers Admitted

Believers let in,
Gardens with rivers below,
Sins forgiven, joy.

There is something that has completely changed my life. I used to be so caught up in the world, always chasing the next thing. Eventually I asked myself, "What is the point of it all? Does any of it really matter in the grand scheme of things?" That is when I started seeking closeness with the Divine. I made it my ultimate goal to get to know Him and to live a life that pleases Him.

I know it sounds heavy, but it has actually made my life so much lighter. Knowing that the Divine is always there, always looking out for me, has given me a peace and optimism that I never knew was possible. I try to strengthen my connection with Him every day by applying lessons of Divine wisdom, performing acts of devotion, constantly surrendering to Him, and just trying to do good in the world. Whatever the results, I make sure to seek forgiveness and return to Him.

Certainly, it is not always easy. I remind myself of the promise of witnessing His majesty, that eternal bliss, that perfect peace. It is real, and it is waiting for those of us who strive to live a life of virtue. The best part is that it is not just about individual salvation. That is why I try to uplift others every day, to help them see the light that I have found. When I face challenges, I hold fast to that connection with everything I have.

I have come to realize that these trials are temporary and that they are actually making me stronger. They are preparing me for the everlasting contentment that awaits beyond this life.

I know this might sound a bit heavy, and I do not mean to preach. However, this journey toward closeness with the Divine has been so transformative for me that I feel compelled to share it. It has given my life a purpose and meaning that I never knew was possible. The best part of it is that anyone can do it. No matter who you are or where you have been, the Divine is always waiting intently. So, if you are feeling lost or empty, if you are asking yourself, "What's the point of it all?" I urge you to seek the Divine. Make Him your ultimate goal, your best friend. Live a life that pleases Him, and hold onto His promise of joy in the hereafter. It is not easy, but it is worth every bit of effort. Trust me, you will never feel alone again.

This whole thing is a process. It is a journey. There are ups and downs, moments of doubt and struggle. Nevertheless, through it all, the Divine is there. He is guiding you, strengthening you, and preparing you for an eternity of bliss in His presence. Along the way, you will find a peace and purpose that you never knew existed. I am not perfect, not by a long shot. I am striving every day to be better, to draw closer to the Divine. On this journey, I have never felt happier or more fulfilled. So, if you are ready to embark on the greatest adventure of your life, if you are willing to put in the work and reap the everlasting rewards, then I urge you to seek the Divine. He is waiting for you, and so is the paradise that He has prepared.

I am not the only one—millions of people around the world have found this same peace and purpose through closeness with the Divine. So, if you are feeling the call, if you are yearning for something more, then do not wait. Start seeking the Divine today. Learn His wisdom, pray, and strive to live a life that pleases Him. And when you mess up, as we all do, do not beat yourself up. Seek forgiveness and keep striving.

I promise you, this journey toward the Divine is the only one that truly matters. It is never too late to start. No matter where you are or what you have done, the Divine is always there, always ready to welcome you home. In His presence, you will find a peace and purpose that lasts forever. I know it sounds too good to be true but trust me, it is real. I have experienced it in my own life, and I have seen it transform countless others. So, what do you say? Are you ready to leave the emptiness behind and embark on the greatest adventure of your life? The journey begins now, and I promise you, it is the only one that truly matters.